QuickCook

QuickCook
Chicken

Recipes by Emma Jane Frost

Every dish, three ways—you choose!
30 minutes | 20 minutes | 10 minutes

An Hachette UK company
www.hachette.co.uk

First published in Great Britain in 2012 by Hamlyn,
a division of Octopus Publishing Group Ltd
Endeavour House, 189 Shaftesbury Avenue, London WC2H 8JY UK
www.octopusbooks.co.uk

Distributed in the US by Hachette Book Group USA
237 Park Avenue, New York, NY 10017 USA
www.octopusbooksusa.com

Distributed in Canada by Canadian Manda Group
165 Dufferin Street, Toronto, Ontario, Canada M6K 3H6

Recipes and text by Emma Jane Frost, Nichola Palmer & Sophie Jones
Copyright © Octopus Publishing Group Ltd 2012

ISBN 978-0-60062-403-5

A CIP catalog record for this book is available from the British Library.

Printed and bound in China

10 9 8 7 6 5 4 3 2 1

Standard level spoon measurements are used in all recipes.

Ovens should be preheated to the specified temperature. If using a convection oven,
follow the manufacturer's instructions for adjusting the time and temperature.
Broilers should also be preheated.

This book includes dishes made with nuts and nut derivatives. It is advisable for
those with known allergic reactions to nuts and nut derivatives and those who may
be potentially vulnerable to these allergies, such as pregnant and nursing mothers,
invalids, the elderly, babies, and children, to avoid dishes made with nuts and nut oils.

It is also prudent to check the labels of pre-prepared ingredients for the possible
inclusion of nut derivatives.

This book contains some dishes made with raw or lightly cooked eggs. It is prudent
for more vulnerable people such as pregnant and nursing mothers, invalids, the
elderly, babies, and young children to avoid uncooked or lightly cooked dishes made
with eggs.

Contents

Introduction

30 20 10—Quick, Quicker, Quickest

This book offers busy cooks a new and flexible approach to planning meals, letting you choose the recipe option that best fits the time you have available. Inside you will find 360 dishes that will inspire and motivate you to get cooking every day of the year. All the recipes take a maximum of 30 minutes to cook. Some take as little as 20 minutes and, amazingly, many take only 10 minutes. With a bit of preparation, you can easily try out one new recipe from this book each night and slowly you will be able to build a wide and exciting portfolio of recipes to suit your needs.

How Does it Work?

Every recipe in the QuickCook series can be cooked one of three ways—a 30-minute version, a 20-minute version, or a super-quick and easy 10-minute version. At the beginning of each chapter you'll find recipes listed by time. Choose a dish based on how much time you have and turn to that page.

You'll find the main recipe in the middle of the page accompanied by a beautiful photograph, as well as two time-variation recipes below.

If you enjoy your chosen dish, why not go back and cook the other time-variation options at a later date? So if you liked the 20-minute Mozzarella Chicken Melts, but only have 10 minutes to spare this time around, you'll find a way to cook it using cheat ingredients or clever shortcuts.

If you love the ingredients and flavors of the 10-minute Chicken Laksa with Noodles, why not try something more substantial, like the 20-minute Stir-Fried Chicken Noodles, or be inspired to make a more elaborate version, like the Thai Chicken Curry? Alternatively, browse through all 360 delicious recipes, find something that catches your eye, and then cook the version that fits your time frame.

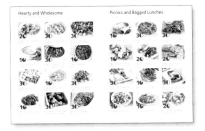

Or, for easy inspiration, turn to the gallery on pages 12–19 to get an instant overview by themes, such as Classics or Hearty and Wholesome.

QuickCook Online

To make life even easier, you can use the special code on each recipe page to email yourself a recipe card for printing, or email a text-only shopping list to your phone. Go to www.hamlynquickcook.com and enter the recipe code at the bottom of each page.

CHI-LIGH-DUC

QuickCook Chicken

Chicken is the most widely consumed meat on the planet. It is relatively inexpensive and quick to cook. Amazingly versatile, its mild flavor makes it a favorite with people of every age.

The unending appeal of chicken as a source of protein lies in its mild flavor, which lends itself to being blended with a host of different ingredients, from the punchy tastes of Mediterranean foods, such as basil and olives, to the rich, heavily spiced stews and curries of India. This is why we find chicken in so many cuisines from around the globe, and why we have been able to include so many exciting and different recipes in this book.

Think of chicken as a blank canvas to which you can add your favorite flavors. Chicken works with almost every style of cooking: Asian-style stir-fries; garlicky or broiled dishes with herbs; richly spiced curries; warm and cold salads; fragrant Thai coconut recipes; coq au vin and other wine-based stews; simple pasta dishes—the options for your evening meal are almost endless.

Tips and Techniques

There a few simple cooking aids that really can have a significant effect on reducing the time spent in the kitchen.

- A food processor and a mini chopper are both really useful, time-saving pieces of equipment.

- A good vegetable peeler, garlic peeler, and a crusher are all great, simple little gadgets to help save time on fiddly jobs.

- Good, sharp knives make food preparation simpler and faster.

- Try cooking large amounts and then freezing in portions. This way, you'll always have a fast, ready-made, low-effort meal ready to simply defrost and cook.

- Preparing ingredients in advance will save time when you cook later on. Peel and chop vegetables, for example, seal them in plastic food bags, and chill until needed.

A Speedy Food

Chicken appeals to cooks for many reasons, not least because it freezes exceptionally well (properly wrapped, a chicken can be frozen with no effect on its flavor or texture for up to two years). But its value as a foundation ingredient in so many dishes can be found in the speed with which it can be cooked. This book offers you an astonishing 360 recipes and variations to choose from, and every one of them can be cooked in half an hour or less. How many other satisfying and tasty foodstuffs are this easy to prepare and cook?

A whole bird, no matter how small, cannot be cooked in less than an hour, of course, but the individual parts of the chicken —a wing, a leg, a thigh, or a breast—should be ready in 30 minutes. It is worth remembering that when you are buying thighs, it pays to buy them already deboned so you can flatten the meat or cut the flesh into chunks and thereby speed up the cooking process. If the recipe calls for the thighs to be kept whole, try to buy smaller thighs because the larger they are the longer they will take to cook. If small or boneless thighs are unavailable, you can speed up the cooking process by making a few fairly deep cuts into the surface of the meat. The same is true of chicken breast. Flatten or score the meat and it will cook much more quickly.

When they are preparing recipes that call for strips of chicken breast, many people choose to use chicken breast tenders. These are usually extremely tender and incredibly easy to cook, so they may be worth the extra money.

With the growth in demand for ready-prepared foods, chicken can now be found in a host of different flavors. If you look in a delicatessen or the cooked meat aisle of a supermarket you can find smoked chicken breast, which is wonderful in salads and on pizzas (try our Smoked Chicken Bruschetta on page 68), Tikka-flavored cooked chicken pieces, which are excellent in sandwiches, and other interesting flavors, including Chinese chicken, barbecue-flavored chicken, and Cajun chicken.

A Healthy Choice

Another reason why chicken breast is such a popular choice is that it contains little fat. Steamed or broiled chicken breast is one of the leanest, healthiest proteins available, and even stir-fried chicken can be low in fat as long as you are careful about the amount of oil you put in the wok or skillet. In our Healthy Feasts chapter you will find a wide array of different recipes that manage to create an abundance of flavor even without a great deal of fat or salt. Remember that a dieter's delight is a cupboard full of strong flavors, such as garlic and ginger, and herbs and spices. Try the delicious Chicken Tikka Kebabs on page 260 or the palette-tingling Chicken with Cashews and Oyster Sauce on page 278.

The key to a successful low-fat diet is to vary the flavors in your meals so you never get bored. In the Healthy Feasts chapter we show you a few tricks, such as how 0 percent fat Greek-style yogurt can be used in place of cream and butter to keep many chicken dishes moist and delicious.

Even though the wings are also technically white meat, you should be aware that they are also the fattiest part of the bird. Be careful when you are barbecuing wings: they are prone to flare up because of the amount of fat released while they are cooking. Chicken thighs and legs are still lean protein when compared to beef, pork, and lamb, however. If you are watching your calorie intake, always remove the chicken skin because the majority of the fat is stored just underneath it.

A Great Choice for Family and Friends

It seems that everybody likes chicken. You can almost guarantee that when you are entertaining a large number of guests, a chicken dish will go down well with everyone. Real winners at parties are the Harrisa Chicken Pilaf (see page 212 in the Food for Friends chapter), which can be served warm or cold. Or, if you want to impress in a hurry you can't fail with our Quick Paella with Artichokes, Chorizo, and Green Beans (see page 216). And if you are hosting a special dinner party, why not try cooking the classic Chicken with a Tarragon Cream Sauce and Mushroom Rice (see page 214)?

Similarly, if you are cooking for a roomful of youngsters, whether aged three or thirteen, chicken recipes are usually well received by most. Try the Chicken Pesto Pasta in our Midweek Meals chapter (see page 76) for a really successful treat or, better still, as a way of introducing children to new flavors through the medium of chicken. How many children could resist the layered Potato, Chicken, Bacon, and Thyme Gratin on page 100? And they would barely notice that they've eaten a whole heap of fabulously iron-rich vegetables when you serve them up a delicious Thick Curried Coconut and Spinach Chicken Soup (see page 142 in the Family Favorites chapter).

So defrost that chicken waiting in the freezer, choose one of our gorgeous recipes, and see how many smiles are in the room when your meal has been eaten. We are certain that no matter which recipe you choose from this book today, it will be a sure-fire winner with everyone.

Spicy

Turn up the heat with this selection of spicy dishes

2 Hoisin Chicken and Bean Sprout Wraps 42

3 Mexican-Style Pasta Salad 56

3 Spiced Chicken Naans 64

2 Thai Red Curry Soup 98

1 Paprika Chicken with Peppers 104

2 Oriental Ground Chicken 106

2 Chicken Chili Pasta 118

2 Spicy Chicken Wings with Avocado Salsa 136

2 Tarragon Chicken Burgers with Spicy Salsa 162

3 Chicken Chili with Potato Wedges and Guacamole 174

1 Piri-Piri Stir-Fry 202

3 Harissa Chicken 212

Fruity

A collection of tasty recipes with fresh fruit flavors

Lemon, Mint, and Chicken Skewers 70

Moroccan Fruity Chicken Stew 78

Coronation Chicken 82

Chicken Biryani 130

Simple Mango and Coconut Curry with Cilantro 172

Chicken Topped with Blue Cheese and Mango Chutney 218

Chicken, Apricot, and Almond Tagine 220

Lime and Chili Chicken with Mashed Sweet Potatoes 246

Saucy Lemon Chicken with Greens 250

Spiced Roast Chicken with Lime 262

Warm Chicken, Pine Nut, and Raisin Salad 266

Herby Quinoa with Lemon and Chicken 268

Classics

Eternally popular classic dishes everyone will love

Caesar Salad with Chicken, Bacon, and Parmesan 52

Cheesy Chicken Omelet 60

Pan-Fried Chicken with Garlicky Mashed Beans 84

Potato, Chicken, Bacon, and Thyme Gratin 100

Chicken Curry in a Hurry 110

Chicken, Broccoli, and Cheese Bake 120

Roasted Chicken Thighs with Roots and Honey 128

Speedy Roast Chicken with Bacon and Stuffing 146

Chicken, Leek, and Parsley Pies 154

Quick Coq au Vin 204

Chicken Minestrone 240

Chicken Ratatouille 258

Taste of the Med

Recipes to savor the flavors of the Mediterranean

Souvlaki 38

Chicken Pesto Pasta 76

Basil, Ricotta, and Sun-Dried Tomato Chicken 94

Tomato, Chicken, Pepper, and Olive Tuscan-Style Tarts 132

Chicken Parmigiana 180

Greek-Style Chicken Thighs with Olives and Green Beans 182

Broiled Gazpacho Chicken Salad 186

Chicken and Fennel Risotto with Vermouth 194

Chicken Koftas 214

Quick Paella with Artichokes, Chorizo, and Green Beans 216

Chicken Roasted with Lemon, Olives, and Saffron 274

Yogurt Chicken with Greek Salad 276

Hearty and Wholesome

Filling and healthy dishes for all the family

Chicken, Chorizo, and Broccoli Pasta 88

Thai Red Curry with Chicken Meatballs 90

Chicken with Potatoes, and Blue Cheese 112

Chicken and Corn Chowder 114

Smoky Cannellini Bean Stew with Sausages and Chicken 122

Chicken and Boston Beans 134

Chicken, Bacon, and Mushroom Pie 138

Thick Curried Coconut and Spinach Soup 142

Chicken Pesto Meatballs in Tomato Sauce with Pasta 158

Lentil and Chicken Stew 164

Roasted Beet, Butternut Squash Wedges, and Thyme Thighs 222

Chicken and Eggplant Bake 242

Picnics and Bagged Lunches

Tasty recipes to transport easily when you're on the run

Chicken Salsa Wraps 24

Fennel, Chicken, and Tomato Pizza 34

Buffalo Chicken Wings with Coleslaw 44

Cajun Chicken and Avocado Melt 46

Chicken, Chorizo, and Sage Skewers 48

Chicken, Basil, and Goat Cheese Panini 54

Chicken, Feta, and Spinach Pasties 96

Simple Warm Chicken Liver Pâté 188

Chicken, Spinach, Onion Chutney, and Goat Cheese Tart 192

Panzanella with Chicken 196

Chicken Couscous Salad 248

Mixed Mushroom, Herb, and Chicken Fritatta 254

Takeout Treats

Recreate your favorite takeout dishes at home

Curried Chicken Samosas 26

Jerk Chicken and Pepper Stir-Fry 32

Chicken Nachos 50

Smoky Barbecue Chicken Pizza 58

Chicken and Rustic Fries 108

Simple Chicken Korma 148

Fajitas 168

Chicken Tacos 234

Chicken Pilau with Cauliflower, Spinach, and Green Beans 244

Baked Chicken and Shrimp Egg Rolls 256

Chicken Tikka Kebabs with Red Onion Relish 260

Chicken with Cashews and Oyster Sauce 278

Batch Cooking

Recipes that can be made in advance and enjoyed later

3

Chicken Quesadillas with
Cilantro and Chile 62

2

Smoked Chicken
Bruschetta 68

1

Chicken Satay 92

3

Crispy Salt and Pepper
Chicken Thighs 102

3

Chicken, Bacon, Vegetable,
and Cheese Layers 144

3

Barbecued Squab Pieces with
Corn and Chile Salsa 150

1

Warm Chicken Ciabatta with
Salsa and Arugula 152

2

Whole-Wheat Chicken Tenders
with Lemon Mayonnaise 156

3

Sticky Soy-Glazed
Drumsticks 170

2

Sesame & Thyme Skewers with
Spicy Mashed Chickpeas 190

3

Chicken Drumstick
Jambalaya 236

2

Spanish Chicken and
Potato Stew 252

QuickCook
Light Bites

Recipes listed by cooking time

10

Chicken Salsa Wraps

Serves 4

2 cups fresh tomato salsa
4 soft flour tortillas
8 oz ready-cooked barbecue-
   flavored chicken, chopped
¼ small red cabbage, shredded
2 carrots, coarsely grated
4 scallions, cut into fine strips
generous ½ cup sour cream
green salad, to serve

- Spoon the tomato salsa onto the tortillas and spread it evenly around. Place one-quarter of the chicken in the center of each one along with some of the cabbage, carrots, and scallions.

- Spoon some sour cream on top and roll up. Cut in half and serve with a green salad.

Chicken Salsa on Baked Potatoes

Cook 4 baking potatoes (each weighing about ¼ lb) in a microwave for 10–15 minutes, or until soft. Meanwhile, mix together 7 oz cooked and chopped barbecue-flavored chicken, ¼ small shredded red cabbage, 2 coarsely grated carrots, and 4 diced scallions. Stir in 4 tablespoons mayonnaise and season with salt and pepper. Cut open the potatoes, fill with the chicken mixture, and spoon some ready-made tomato salsa on top to serve.

Balsamic Chicken Wraps

Thinly slice 3 boneless, skinless chicken breasts and coat in a mixture of 2 tablespoons balsamic vinegar, 2 tablespoons olive oil, and 1 crushed garlic clove. Season with salt and pepper. Cook the chicken, in batches, under a hot broiler or in a skillet for 1–2 minutes on each side until cooked through. Place on warmed soft flour tortillas with 2 cups tomato salsa, ¼ small shredded red cabbage, 2 grated carrots, and 4 scallions, cut into strips. Top with sour cream, roll up, and serve.

CHI-LIGH-KER

Curried Chicken Samosas

Serves 4

½ lb potatoes, finely diced
¾ cup frozen mixed vegetables
   (such as peas, whole kernel
   sweet corn, and diced carrots)
7 oz cooked chicken, chopped
1 tablespoon medium curry paste
1 tablespoon mango chutney
8 sheets of filo pastry, thawed if
   frozen, halved lengthwise
1 tablespoon sunflower oil
1 tablespoon poppy seeds
mango chutney, to serve

- Cook the potatoes in lightly salted boiling water for 5 minutes, adding the frozen vegetables toward the end so they thaw.

- Meanwhile, mix together the chicken, curry paste, and mango chutney. Drain the vegetables, add to the chicken, and mix well.

- Place 2 tablespoons of the mixture in the corner of half a sheet of filo pastry. Fold the end of the pastry over the filling to make a triangle, then continue folding along the pastry, keeping the triangular shape until the pastry is used up. Place on a cookie sheet and repeat with remaining filling and pastry to make 8 samosas.

- Brush the tops of the samosas with oil, scatter with poppy seeds, and bake in the preheated oven at 400°F for 15 minutes, or until golden and crisp. Serve with mango chutney.

---

1 Curried Chicken and Rice

Combine an 8 oz package of ready-cooked basmati rice with 1 tablespoon medium curry paste and 1 tablespoon mango chutney. Add 7 oz cooked chopped chicken and 1 cup frozen mixed vegetables. Heat in a microwave for 5 minutes until hot. Serve with extra mango chutney and poppadoms.

2   Curried Chicken Puffs

Cut a puff pastry sheet into 4 squares. In a bowl mix together 7 oz cooked chopped chicken, 1 tablespoon medium curry paste, and 1 tablespoon mango chutney. Add ½ lb finely diced potatoes (about 1½ cups) and a handful of canned whole kernel sweet corn. Place the filling on one triangular half of each pastry square. Brush the edges with a little beaten egg and fold the pastry over to make triangles, pressing down well to seal. Place on a cookie sheet, brush with egg, and bake in a preheated oven at 400°F for 10 minutes, or until well risen and golden. Serve warm with mango chutney.

Creamy Herby Chicken with Mushrooms on Bagels

Serves 4

4 bagels, halved

2 tablespoons ready-made garlic butter, softened

2 tablespoons olive oil

1 small onion, chopped

2 skinless, boneless chicken breasts, sliced

2¾ cups crimini mushrooms, quartered

2 tablespoons sherry

1 scant cup crème fraîche

2 tablespoons chopped parsley

salt and pepper

- Place the bagel halves, cut-side up, on a cookie sheet. Butter them with the garlic butter and bake in a preheated oven at 375°F for 10–15 minutes, or until crisp.

- Meanwhile, put the oil in a skillet over medium heat, add the onion, and cook for 3 minutes. Add the chicken and cook for 5 minutes. Then add the mushrooms and cook for a further 5 minutes, or until tender. Add the sherry and allow to bubble, then stir in the crème fraîche and parsley and season with salt and pepper. Simmer, stirring, adding a little water if the mixture is too thick. Spoon the mixture onto the baked bagels and serve.

---

1 **Creamy Chicken and Mushrooms on Toast** Fry 1½ cups sliced mushrooms in 2 tablespoons ready-made garlic butter for 3 minutes until tender. Stir in a 14 oz package of chicken in cream sauce and heat, stirring, for a few minutes until hot. Stir in 1 tablespoon chopped parsley and spoon onto hot buttered toast to serve.

2 **Garlic Baked Mushrooms with Chicken** Put 4 large portobello mushrooms, stalk-side up, on a cookie sheet. Dot with 2 tablespoons ready-made garlic butter, season with salt and pepper, and bake in a preheated oven at 400°F for 15 minutes, or until tender. Meanwhile, fry 1 small onion and 2 chopped skinless, boneless chicken breasts in 1 tablespoon olive oil for 5 minutes. Stir in 1 scant cup crème fraîche and 2 tablespoons chopped parsley. Season with salt and pepper and simmer for 5 minutes, adding a little water if the mixture becomes too thick. Spoon onto the baked garlicky mushrooms to serve.

Chicken, Zucchini, and Bacon Kebabs

Serves 4

16 slices bacon

2 zucchini, each cut into
8 chunks

3 skinless, boneless chicken
breasts, each cut into 8 pieces

1 tablespoon sunflower oil

2 tablespoons clear honey

1 tablespoon wholegrain mustard

whole kernel sweet corn and
peas, to serve

- Stretch each slice of bacon with the back of a knife. Cut each slice in half and wrap around a piece of zucchini. Thread onto 8 skewers, alternating the zucchini with pieces of chicken.

- Place the kebabs on a foil-lined broiler pan. Warm the oil, honey, and mustard together in a small pan, then brush it all over the kebabs. Place the pan under a preheated medium broiler for 10 minutes, turning occasionally and brushing with any remaining honey mixture until the bacon is crisp and the chicken is cooked. Serve with corn and peas.

10 Chicken, Bacon, and Zucchini

Baguette Cut 2 zucchini into slices lengthwise and place on a foil-lined broiler pan. Brush the zucchini with a little oil, honey, and mustard and broil together with 4 slices of bacon for about 5 minutes, or until the zucchini slices are tender and the bacon is crisp. Cut a baguette into 4 pieces and cut in half lengthwise. Butter it and fill it with 8 oz cooked sliced chicken and the zucchini and bacon.

30 Chicken, Bacon, and Zucchini

Kebabs with Corn Fritters
Prepare the kebabs as above. Put 4 tablespoons self-rising flour in a bowl with a pinch of salt. Whisk in 2 eggs to make a smooth batter. Drain a 15 oz can whole sweet corn kernels and add to the batter. Heat 2 tablepoons sunflower oil in a large skillet over medium heat, add the mixture a spoonful at a time, and cook for 2 minutes until set and golden underneath.

Turn the fritters over and cook for a further 2 minutes. Repeat with remaining mixture and serve with the kebabs.

Jerk Chicken and Pepper Stir-Fry

Serves 4

1 tablespoon sunflower oil

8 chicken drumsticks

1 red pepper, cored, seeded, and cut into chunks

1 green pepper, cored, seeded, and cut into chunks

¼ lb sugar snap peas

1 mango, seed removed and flesh diced

juice of 1 lime

2½ cups rich chicken stock

1 tablespoon sunflower oil

For the jerk paste

1 red onion, roughly diced

1 teaspoon dried thyme

½ teaspoon ground allspice

½ teaspoon ground cinnamon

1 bell chile, roughly diced

salt and pepper

- To make the jerk paste, put all the paste ingredients in a small food processor or blender and process to make a smooth paste.

- Cut a few slashes across the thickest part of each drumstick. Rub the drumsticks with the paste, pushing it into the slashes.

- Heat the oil in a large deep skillet over high heat. Add the chicken drumsticks and peppers and fry for 5 minutes, turning occasionally. Add the sugar snap peas, mango, lime juice, and stock and bring to a boil. Reduce the heat, cover, and simmer for 15 minutes, turning the chicken occasionally until cooked through. Serve with rice.

---

1 Jerk Chicken Burgers

Slice 2 skinless, boneless chicken breasts in half horizontally. Season and fry in 1 tablespoon sunflower oil for 5 minutes, turning once, or until cooked through. Serve in hamburger buns with ready-made jerk sauce and crisp lettuce.

2 Jerk Chicken with Rice and Peas

Heat a 13½ fl oz can coconut milk in a pan with 2 cups water over medium hest. Add 1 cup plus 2 tablespoons quick-cooking long-grain rice, a 15 oz can rinsed and drained kidney beans, and 1 teaspoon dried thyme. Bring to a boil, reduce the heat, cover, and simmer for

15 minutes, or until the rice is tender and most of the liquid has been absorbed. Meanwhile, toss 4 sliced skinless, boneless chickens fillets in 1 tablespoon jerk seasoning mix. Stir-fry the chicken in 1 tablespoon sunflower oil for 5 minutes, or until cooked through. Serve with rice and peas and some lime wedges on the side.

 # Fennel, Chicken, and Tomato Pizza

Serves 2

2 tablespoons olive oil
1 small onion, sliced
1 garlic clove, crushed
3 tomatoes, diced
pinch of sugar
1 tablespoon tomato paste
4½ oz pizza crust mix
1 small head of fennel, thinly
   sliced
¼ lb cooked chicken, chopped
8 cherry tomatoes, halved
5 oz mozzarella cheese, sliced
salt and pepper

- Heat the olive oil in a skillet over medium heat, add the onion, garlic, and fennel and cook for 3 minutes. Add the tomatoes, sugar, and tomato paste and simmer for 5 minutes, or until the mixture is soft and pulpy. Season with salt and pepper.

- Meanwhile, make the pizza crust according to the instructions on the package. Knead lightly until smooth, shape into a ball, and roll out thinly to a circle about 12 inches across. Place on a cookie sheet.

- Spread the tomato and fennel sauce over the pizza base and scatter with the chicken and cherry tomatoes. Arrange the mozzarella on top and bake in a preheated oven at 425°F for 15 minutes, or until crisp and golden.

1 Chicken and Fennel Pizza

Cover a piece of garlic and herb flat bread with ready-made pizza topping sauce, thin slices from a small fennel head, and ¼ lb chopped cooked chicken. Arrange 5 oz sliced mozzarella cheese on top and bake in a preheated oven at 425°F for 10 minutes.

2 Fennel, Chicken, and Tomato Pasta

Heat 2 tablespoons olive oil in a pan, add 1 diced onion, 1 crushed garlic clove, ½ lb chopped cooked chicken, and 1 small, diced head of fennel. Cook for 3 minutes, then add 3 diced tomatoes and ¾ cup passata. Season with salt and pepper and stir in a handful of black olives. Serve with freshly cooked pasta.

 # Parmesan Chicken Scallops

Serves 4

2 skinless, boneless chicken breasts, halved horizontally

2 tablespoons all-purpose flour

1 egg, beaten

2½ cups fresh ciabatta bread crumbs

¾ cup freshly grated Parmesan cheese

3 tablespoons sunflower oil

4 small baguettes, cut in half lengthwise

4 tablespoons mayonnaise

4 small handfuls mixed salad leaves

salt and pepper

- Place the chicken halves between 2 pieces of plastic wrap and beat with a rolling pin to flatten slightly. Put the flour on a plate and the egg in a wide, flat bowl. On a separate plate mix together the bread crumbs and Parmesan and season with salt and pepper.

- Lightly coat each piece of chicken in the flour, shaking off any excess, dip into the beaten egg, and then roll in the bread crumb mixture to coat, pressing the crumbs on firmly.

- Heat the oil in a large skillet over medium heat, add the chicken, and cook for about 5 minutes, turning once, until golden, crisp, and cooked through.

- Spread mayonnaise onto the cut sides of the baguette then add the salad leaves and hot chicken to serve.

1 Chicken Caesar Baguette

Stir-fry 2 skinless, boneless chicken breasts, cut into strips, in 2 tablespoons sunflower oil for about 5 minutes, or until cooked through. Pile onto slices of French bread along with mixed salad leaves. Drizzle with Caesar salad dressing to serve.

3 Baked Pesto Parmesan Chicken with Sweet Potato Wedges

Cut 4 scrubbed sweet potatoes into wedges. Toss them in 4 tablespoons olive oil and then season with salt and pepper. Spread out on a cookie sheet and bake in a preheated oven at 425°F for 25 minutes, turning occasionally, until golden and tender. Meanwhile, cut 2 skinless, boneless chicken breasts in half horizontally. Coat them in pesto sauce and then with a layer of 2½ cups fresh white bread crumbs mixed with ¾ cups freshly grated Parmesan cheese. Place the chicken on a cookie sheet and drizzle with 3 tablespoons sunflower oil. Bake in the oven with the sweet potatoes for 15 minutes, or until crisp and cooked through. Serve with mayonnaise and mixed salad leaves.

 Souvlaki

Serves 4

3 tablespoons olive oil
3 tablespoons red wine
1 teaspoon dried oregano
finely grated zest and juice of
   1 lemon
1 garlic clove, crushed
4 skinless, boneless chicken
   breasts, cut into strips
4 pita breads, warmed and split
   open
salt and pepper

To serve

cabbage, shredded
cucumber, diced
tomato, diced
chili sauce

- In a large bowl mix together the olive oil, wine, oregano, lemon zest and juice, and garlic. Season with salt and pepper, add the chicken, mix well, and leave to marinate for 15 minutes.

- Thread the chicken onto skewers and place on a foil-lined broiler pan. Cook under a preheated hot broiler for 8–10 minutes, turning occasionally, until the chicken is cooked and beginning to char at the edges.

- Slide the chicken off of the skewers into the warm pita bread followed by some shredded cabbage, diced cucumber, diced tomato, and a dash of chili sauce.

Hot Chicken and Hummus Pita Pockets Stir-fry ½ lb chicken tenders in 1 tablespoon olive oil with ½ teaspoon dried oregano, 1 teaspoon garlic paste, and the grated zest of ½ lemon for 5 minutes, or until cooked. Warm 4 pita breads, cut in half widthwise, and open slightly to form pockets. Stuff some chicken along with 4 tablespoons ready-made hummus and crisp romaine lettuce into each pocket to serve.

 Pan-Fried Lemon Chicken with Zucchini Thinly slice 4 skinless, boneless chicken breasts and toss them in a mixture of 3 tablespoons olive oil, 3 tablespoons red wine, 1 teaspoon dried oregano, the finely grated zest and juice of 1 lemon, and 2 crushed garlic cloves. Leave to marinate for 15 minutes. Pan-fry the chicken in a hot skillet with 2 tablespoons olive oil and 2 zucchini cut into thin sticks for 5 minutes, or until golden. Add the marinade and cook for a few minutes to reduce slightly. Serve with rice.

Smoked Chicken, Asparagus, and Blue Cheese Calzone

Serves 2

6 oz asparagus spears, trimmed and cut into 1 inch pieces

4½ oz pizza crust mix

1 smoked cooked chicken breast, sliced

4 oz Roquefort cheese, crumbled

- Cook the asparagus in lightly salted boiling water for 3 minutes until just tender, then drain.

- Meanwhile, make the pizza crust according to the instructions on the package. Knead lightly until smooth then roll out thinly to make a large circle, about 12 inches across, then place on a cookie sheet.

- Scatter the chicken, asparagus, and crumbled cheese onto half the dough, leaving a ½ inch border. Brush the edges with water and fold the dough over to cover the filling, pressing the edges firmly to seal. Bake in a preheated oven at 425°F for 15 minutes until crisp and golden. Serve warm.

1 Smoked Chicken, Asparagus, and Blue Cheese Salad Put 5 oz mixed salad leaves in a bowl. Add 1 sliced smoked chicken breast, 6 oz lightly cooked asparagus spears, and a handful of pine nuts. Drizzle with ready-made blue cheese salad dressing and toss lightly to mix.

2 Smoked Chicken and Asparagus Tarts Cook 6 oz trimmed and halved asparagus spears in lightly salted boiling water for 3 minutes, then drain. Unroll half a sheet of ready-rolled puff pastry and cut it into 2 rectangles. Place on a baking pan and divide the topping between the 2 tarts, each with half of a sliced smoked chicken breast, the asparagus, and 4 oz crumbled Roquefort cheese. Bake in a preheated oven at 425°F for 10–15 minutes, or until well risen and golden.

Hoisin Chicken and Bean Sprout Wraps

Serves 4

1 tablespoon vegetable oil

3 skinless, boneless chicken breasts, cut into strips

2 tablespoons hoisin sauce, plus extra for dipping

½ teaspoon ginger paste

2 teaspoons dark soy sauce

8 rice-flour pancakes (the type served with crispy duck)

1¼ cups bean sprouts

4 scallions, cut into thin strips

¼ cucumber, cut into thin strips

- Heat the oil in a wok or skillet over high heat, add the chicken, and fry for 5 minutes, or until cooked through. Add the hoisin sauce, ginger paste, and soy sauce and stir-fry until the sauce is sticky and coats the chicken. Remove from the heat.

- Warm the pancakes in a microwave or in an oven at 325°F according to the instructions on the package. Divide the bean sprouts, scallions, and cucumber among the pancakes, place some chicken on top, and roll up. Serve with extra hoisin sauce for dipping.

10 Hoisin Chicken Rice Noodle Salad

Coat about ¾ lb chicken tenders in a 4 oz pouch ready-made hoisin and garlic stir-fry sauce. Stir-fry in 1 tablespoon sunflower oil for about 5 minutes, or until cooked. Meanwhile, soak 7 oz vermicelli rice noodles in boiling water for a few minutes until softened. Drain, mix with the cooked chicken and toss with 7 oz mixed oriental salad greens to serve.

30 Hoisin Chicken Parcels

In a large bowl mix together 2 tablespoons hoisin sauce, ½ teaspoon ginger paste, and 2 teaspoons dark soy sauce. Add 2 thinly sliced skinless, boneless chicken breasts, 4 scallions, cut into strips, 1¼ cups bean sprouts and 1 large carrot, cut into strips. Divide the mixture among 4 large squares of double thickness wax paper. Fold the paper over the filling, twisting the edges to form a parcel. Place on a cookie sheet and cook in a preheated oven at 400°F for 20 minutes. Serve with freshly cooked noodles.

Buffalo Chicken Wings with Coleslaw

Serves 4

2 tablespoons clear honey
5 tablespoons tomato ketchup
2 teaspoons English mustard
2 teaspoons Worcestershire sauce
½–1 teaspoon hot chili sauce
2 tablespoons sunflower oil
2 lb chicken wings

For the coleslaw

4 tablespoons mayonnaise
2 tablespoons lemon juice
¾ lb white cabbage, finely shredded
1 small red onion, coarsely grated
1 medium carrot, coarsely grated
1 tablespoon chopped parsley
pepper

- In a large bowl mix together the honey, ketchup, mustard, Worcestershire sauce, chili sauce, and oil. Add the chicken wings and mix well to coat.

- Put the chicken wings on a large, foil-lined baking pan and bake in a preheated oven at 400°F for 25 minutes, turning occasionally and brushing with any remaining sauce in the bowl, until cooked through.

- Meanwhile, make the coleslaw. Mix together the ingredients and season with pepper. Serve the chicken wings with the coleslaw on the side.

1 Spicy Chicken and Corn

Reheat 1½ lb ready-cooked and spicy-flavored chicken wings in a microwave according to the instructions on the package. Serve with corn on the cob boiled in lightly salted water for 5–8 minutes until tender. Scatter with dried red pepper flakes and spread with butter to serve.

2 Barbecue Chicken with Blue Cheese Dip and Celery

 Cut 4 skinless, boneless chicken breasts into strips. Coat in a mixture of 1 tablespoon clear honey, 2½ tablespoons tomato ketchup, 1 teaspoon English mustard, 1 teaspoon Worcestershire sauce, a dash of hot chili sauce, and 1 tablespoon sunflower oil. Arrange the chicken pieces on a foil-lined broiler pan and broil, turning occasionally, for 5–10 minutes, or until cooked through. Meanwhile, using a fork, mash together ¾ cup sour cream and 2 oz crumbled blue cheese. Serve the chicken with the blue cheese dip and celery sticks.

Cajun Chicken and Avocado Melt

Serves 2

1 small ciabatta loaf, halved lengthwise

2 tablespoons tomato chutney

2 tomatoes, sliced

3½ oz ready-cooked Cajun-spiced chicken breast, sliced

1 small avocado, sliced

5 oz mozzarella cheese, drained and sliced

- Put the ciabatta halves, cut-side down, on a foil-lined broiler pan and toast under a preheated medium broiler for a few minutes until crisp and hot. Turn the bread halves over and spread with the tomato chutney. Arrange the tomato slices on top, followed by the chicken, avocado, and finally the mozzarella.

- Place under the broiler and cook for 5 minutes, or until the cheese has melted and the topping is hot.

Cajun Chicken Burgers

Cut 2 skinless, boneless chicken breasts in half horizontally and dust with 1 teaspoon Cajun seasoning mix. Fry in 1 tablespoon sunflower oil for 5 minutes, turning once, until golden and cooked through. Place on toasted hamburger buns and add slices of tomato and avocado. Spoon on some tomato salsa and sour cream to serve.

Cajun Chicken "Rarebit"

Mix together 1½ cups grated sharp cheddar cheese, 1 teaspoon Cajun seasoning mix, a pinch of cayenne pepper, ½ beaten egg, and 1 tablespoon beer. Toast 2 large slices of crusty bread and place 1 cooked, sliced chicken breast and 2 sliced tomatoes on top of each. Cover with the cheese mixture and cook under the broiler until golden and bubbling.

Chicken, Chorizo, and Sage Skewers

Serves 4

4 skinless, boneless chicken thighs, each cut into 4 pieces
4 small cooking chorizo, halved
12 sage leaves
1 tablespoon olive oil
2 teaspoon wholegrain mustard

To serve

baby spinach leaves
crusty bread

- Thread the chicken, chorizo, and sage leaves onto 4 metal skewers. Whisk together the olive oil and wholegrain mustard and brush over the skewers.

- Cook on a hot ridged griddle pan or under a preheated hot broiler for 10–15 minutes, turning occasionally and brushing with more mustard mixture until the chicken and chorizo are cooked.

- Slide the chicken and chorizo off of the skewers and serve with baby spinach leaves and crusty bread.

Chicken and Chorizo Pasta

Cook 12 oz quick-cook pasta shapes in a pan of lightly salted boiling water for 5–8 minutes, or until al dente. Meanwhile, fry 3 oz sliced chorizo in a dry skillet for 2 minutes. Add 1½ cups tomato pasta sauce from a jar and 6 oz cooked chopped chicken. Heat through, drain the pasta, and add to the sauce. Mix well and serve with freshly grated Parmesan cheese.

Quick Roast Chicken with Chorizo and Potatoes

Toss 4 halved skinless, boneless chicken thighs and 8 small cooking chorizo (weighing 3 oz each) in a mixture of 1 tablespoon olive oil and 2 teaspoons wholegrain mustard. Place in a roasting pan with ¾ lb baby new potatoes and 3 whole unpeeled garlic cloves. Drizzle with 2 more tablespoons olive oil, season with salt and pepper, and bake in a preheated oven at 400°F for 25 minutes, or until golden and tender. Meanwhile, fry 1 diced onion and 1 crushed garlic clove in 1 tablespoon olive oil over medium heat for 5 minutes until softened. Add 1¼ cups canned diced tomatoes and 1 tablespoon tomato paste. Simmer, stirring occasionally, until thickened. Serve the sauce with the chicken, chorizo, and potatoes.

Chicken Nachos

Serves 4

6 soft corn tortillas
1 tablespoon sunflower oil
½ teaspoon sea salt flakes
3 tomatoes, diced
1 red chile, seeded and finely
   chopped
1 tablespoon chopped fresh
   cilantro
juice of 1 lime
½ lb cooked chicken, chopped
½ cup jalapeño slices from a jar,
   drained
¾ cup cheddar cheese, grated
salt and pepper
fresh cilantro leaves, to garnish
¾ cup sour cream, to serve

- Brush the tortillas with oil, sprinkle with sea salt, and cut into triangles. Spread them out on 2 cookie sheets and bake in a preheated oven at 375°F for 8–10 minutes, or until crisp. Transfer to a wire rack to cool while you make the salsa.

- Mix together the tomatoes, chile, cilantro, and lime juice. Season with salt and pepper.

- Scatter the chicken onto the baked tortillas, along with the jalapeño slices and diced tomato mixture then cover with a layer of grated cheddar. Return to the oven for 3–4 minutes to allow the cheese to melt. Garnish with cilantro leaves and serve with sour cream.

Quick-Assembly Nachos

Spread 7 oz tortilla chips in the bottom of an ovenproof dish. Arrange ½ lb chopped cooked chicken and ½ cup jalapeño slices from a jar on top. Dot with spoonfuls of ready-made salsa then scatter ¾ cup grated cheddar cheese over everything. Place under a medium-hot broiler for 5 minutes, or until the cheese melts. Serve with sour cream.

Burritos

Mix together 3 finely diced tomatoes, 1 finely diced red chile, 1 tablespoon chopped fresh cilantro, and the juice of 1 lime. Spoon the mixture down the center of 4 soft flour tortillas. Place spoonfuls of ready-made guacamole, ½ lb chopped cooked chicken, and ½ cup jalapeño slices from a jar on top. Fold a 1 inch strip of tortilla over at the bottom of the filling, turn the tortilla 90 degrees, and roll it up. Hold each roll in place with a toothpick to serve.

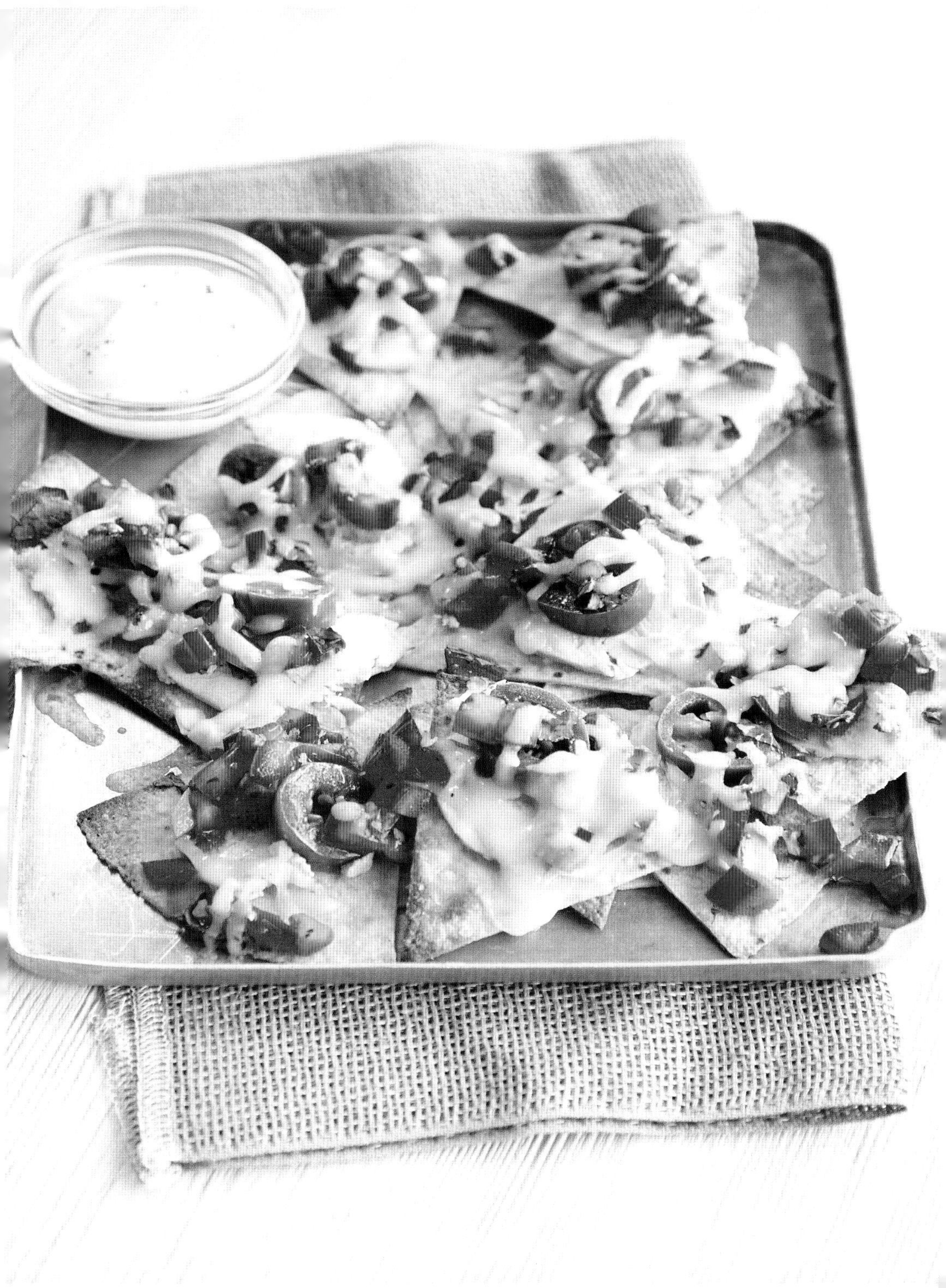

Caesar Salad with Chicken, Bacon, and Parmesan

Serves 4

½ ciabatta loaf, cubed

2 tablespoons olive oil

1 romaine lettuce, leaves
separated and roughly torn

½ lb cooked chicken, chopped

3 slices bacon cooked until crisp
then broken into pieces

6 tablespoons ready-made
Caesar salad dressing

generous ¼ cup Parmesan cheese
shavings

- Place the ciabatta cubes on a foil-lined broiler pan and drizzle with the olive oil. Place under a preheated medium broiler for about 5 minutes, turning occasionally, until golden and crisp, but keeping an eye on them so they don't burn.

- Meanwhile, add the lettuce leaves to a salad bowl with the chicken and most of the bacon pieces.

- Add the toasted bread cubes and salad dressing and toss well to coat. Scatter with the reserved bacon pieces and the Parmesan shavings and serve.

2 Chicken Caesar and Croutons

Cut ½ ciabatta loaf into cubes. Mix 1 crushed garlic clove and 4 tablespoons olive oil and toss the cubes in the oil. Spread on a cookie sheet and bake in a preheated oven at 400°F for 10 minutes, or until crisp. Scatter them over a bowl of torn romaine lettuce leaves, chopped cooked chicken, and crisp bacon pieces tossed in ready-made Caesar salad dressing.

3 Caesar Salad with Homemade

Dressing Cut ½ ciabatta loaf into cubes, place on a cookie sheet, and drizzle with 2 tablespoons olive oil. Bake in a preheated oven at 400°F for 15 minutes, or until crisp and golden. Meanwhile, make the dressing. In a bowl mix together 3 tablespoons mayonnaise, ¼ cup freshly grated Parmesan cheese, 1 tablespoon lemon juice, 2 tablespoons water, a dash of

Worcestershire sauce, and 1 finely chopped anchovy fillet from a can. Put the torn leaves of 1 romaine lettuce in a bowl. Add ½ lb cooked chopped chicken, 3 slices bacon that has cooked until crisp and then broken into pieces, and the bread cubes. Toss together with the dressing and serve.

Chicken, Basil, and Goat Cheese Panini

Serves 4

4 tablespoons pesto

1 tablespoon olive oil

4 panini rolls or 4 part-baked baguettes, halved

2 cooked chicken breasts, sliced

1 generous cup sun-dried tomatoes in oil, drained

7 oz goat cheese, sliced

handful of fresh basil leaves

- Mix together the pesto and oil and brush it over the cut side of the bottom halves of the panini rolls or baguettes. Place the sliced chicken, sun-dried tomatoes, goat cheese, and basil on top of the layer of pesto. Cover with the top half of the rolls or baguettes.

- Cook in a sandwich press or panini griddler for about 5 minutes, or until the bread is crisp and filling is hot. Alternatively, cook in a hot skillet or ridged griddle pan, pressing the rolls down firmly before turning and cooking on the other side.

Chicken and Goat Cheese Salad

Mix together a 3½ oz bag of mixed salad leaves, 2 cooked sliced chicken breasts, 2 cups diced sun-dried tomatoes, 7 oz sliced goat cheese, and a handful of black olives. Whisk 1 tablespoon pesto with 1 tablespoon olive oil and drizzle it over the salad to serve.

Chicken and Goat Cheese Pizza

Spread 4 tablespoons tomato pizza topping sauce evenly onto a large ready-made pizza crust. Arrange 2 cooked and sliced chicken breasts, 4 oz sliced goat cheese, and a handful of black olives on top. Whisk together 1 tablespoon pesto with 1 tablespoon olive oil, drizzle the mixture over the pizza, and bake in a preheated oven at 400°F for 15 minutes, or until the crust is crisp and the topping is hot.

Mexican-Style Pasta Salad

Serves 4

8 oz pasta shapes, such as fusilli

1 red pepper, cored, seeded, and halved

1 orange pepper, cored, seeded, and halved

7 oz cooked Cajun-style chicken, cut into bite-size pieces

1 cup canned mixed chili beans

1 avocado, chopped

handful of fresh cilantro leaves, roughly chopped

For the dressing

¾ cup sour cream

finely grated zest and juice of 1 lime

½ teaspoon Cajun seasoning mix

- Cook the pasta in lightly salted boiling water for about 10 minutes, or until al dente. Drain, rinse under cold running water, and drain again.

- Meanwhile, put the peppers under a hot broiler for 8–10 minutes, turning once until softened and the skin is beginning to char. Transfer the peppers to a bowl, cover with plastic wrap, and set aside for 5 minutes.

- Make the dressing. Whisk together the sour cream, lime zest and juice, and Cajun seasoning.

- Transfer the drained pasta to a large salad bowl. Add the cooked chicken, beans, avocado, and cilantro. Remove the skins from the peppers, roughly chop the flesh, and add to the salad. Drizzle the dressing over everything and lightly toss together.

1 Mexican-Style Open Sandwich

Arrange some slices of cooked Cajun-style chicken, sliced tomatoes, sliced avocado, fresh cilantro leaves, and sour cream dressing onto 4 slices of rustic whole-wheat bread and serve.

2 Fruity Mexican Chicken Salad

Cook 8 oz pasta shapes in lightly salted boiling water for 10 minutes, or until al dente. Drain, rinse under cold running water, and drain again. Mix the pasta with 7 oz cooked Cajun-style chicken, 4 oz roasted red peppers from a jar, 1 peeled and diced mango, and a handful of fresh cilantro leaves. Drizzle with the sour cream dressing as above and serve.

 # Smoky Barbecued Chicken Pizza

Serves 4

2 cups all-purpose flour

½ teaspoon salt

1 teaspoon baking soda

pinch of sugar

2 tablespoons cold butter

¾ cup buttermilk or plain yogurt

4 tablespoons tomato pizza topping sauce

½ lb cooked chicken, chopped

2 tablespoons smoky barbecue sauce

4 oz roasted peppers from a jar, chopped

5 oz mozzarella cheese, sliced

- Sift the flour into a bowl with the salt, baking soda, and sugar. Coarsely grate the butter into the mixture. Stir well to break up any clumps of butter, add the buttermilk or yogurt, and mix to a soft dough.

- Knead the dough lightly until smooth, shape into a ball, and pat out with your hands to a large circle about 12 inches across. Place on a cookie sheet or pizza pan.

- Spread the pizza sauce over the dough, leaving a small border around the edge. Mix together the chicken and barbecue sauce and spread onto the pizza. Arrange the peppers and mozzarella on top and bake in a preheated oven at 400°F for 15 minutes, or until the crust is cooked and the topping is golden.

Barbecued Chicken and Sweet Corn Pizza Muffins Cut 4 English muffins in half, put them on a foil-lined broiler pan, and toast under the broiler on both sides. Chop ½ lb cooked chicken and mix with 2½ cups whole sweet corn kernels then stir in 3 tablespoons smoky barbecue sauce. Spoon onto the toasted muffins, cover evenly with 1 cup grated sharp cheddar cheese, and broil until the cheese is melted and bubbling and serve.

 Thin and Crispy Pizza with Chicken in Barbecue Sauce Unroll a ready-rolled sheet of shortcrust pastry and place on a cookie sheet. Spread 4 tablespoons pizza topping sauce over the top. Chop ½ lb cooked chicken, mix it with 2 tablespoons smoky barbecue sauce and scatter on top of the pastry. Chop 4 oz roasted red peppers from a jar, slice 5 oz mozzarella cheese, and arrange them on top. Bake in a preheated oven at 400°F for 15 minutes or until crisp and golden.

Cheesy Chicken Omelet

Serves 2

4 eggs
1 tablespoon butter
3 oz cooked chicken, chopped
scant ½ cup grated Gruyère
   cheese
salt and pepper
salad, to serve

- Put a small nonstick skillet on the stove to heat. Crack the eggs into a bowl, season with salt and pepper, and add 1 tablespoon cold water. Beat with a fork until evenly mixed.

- Add the butter to the skillet. When it is foaming and melted pour in the beaten egg mixture. As the eggs begin to set, use a wooden spoon to draw the mixture into the center of the skillet, allowing the runny egg to flow to the outer edge.

- When the top of the omelet is softly set arrange the chicken and cheese down the center. Starting at the side nearest the handle, flip the omelet over the filling and then tip it out on to a plate. Cut in half and serve with a simple salad.

Frittata

Beat together 4 eggs and season with salt and pepper. Heat 1 tablespoon olive oil in a small skillet with a heatproof handle. Add 1¼ cups diced cooked potatoes and fry for 5 minutes until golden. Add 2 diced scallions, 3 oz chopped cooked chicken, and a handful of frozen peas. Heat through, then pour the eggs over the mixture. Cook until just set. Arrange 2 oz sliced Gruyère on top and broil until the frittata is just firm and the cheese has melted.

Soufflé Omelet

Separate 4 eggs. Season the egg yolks and whisk the egg whites until they form soft peaks. Lightly fold the egg whites into the egg yolks. Melt 1 tablespoon butter in a large skillet. When it is foaming add the egg mixture and spread it out evenly. When it is lightly set arrange 3 oz chopped cooked chicken and 2 oz sliced Gruyère cheese on the top. Place the skillet under a medium broiler until the egg is set and the cheese has melted. Fold the omelet over and slide it out onto a plate. Serve with tomato salad.

Chicken Quesadillas with Cilantro and Chile

Serves 4

8 soft flour tortillas
1 cup canned refried beans
½ lb cooked chicken, chopped
1 red chile, seeded and minced
4 tomatoes, finely diced
handful of fresh cilantro leaves,
  roughly chopped
1½ cups sharp cheddar cheese,
  grated
3 tablespoons olive oil
lettuce and whole kernel sweet
  corn salad, to serve

- Spread the refried beans onto 4 of the tortillas then place some cooked chicken, diced chile, tomatoes, cilantro, and grated cheese on top. Cover with the remaining tortillas, pressing them together firmly.

- Heat 1 tablespoon olive oil in a large skillet, add one quesadilla, and fry for 3 minutes on each side, or until the cheese has melted and the quesadilla is golden and crisp. Remove from the pan and keep warm. Repeat with the remaining quesadillas, adding a little more oil as necessary.

- Cut into wedges and serve warm with crisp lettuce tossed with whole kernel sweet corn.

Chile Chicken Nachos

Spread 5 oz tortilla chips over the bottom of a large ovenproof dish. Dollop spoonfuls of 1 cup canned refried beans onto the chips, scatter with 6 oz chopped cooked chicken, then spread 4 tablespoons spicy tomato salsa on top. Scatter with 1 cup grated cheddar cheese and place under a medium broiler until the cheese melts. Scatter with chopped cilantro and serve.

Chicken and Chile Wraps

Spread 4 tomato-flavored soft flour tortilla wraps with 1 cup canned refried beans. Chop ½ lb cooked chicken and place evenly down the center of each tortilla. Spread 1 minced red chile, 3 diced tomatoes, and a handful of roughly chopped fresh cilantro leaves on top. Cover with a layer of 1½ cups grated cheddar cheese and roll up. Cut each wrap in half and arrange in an ovenproof dish. Scatter a little extra cheese on top of the wraps. Place in the preheated oven at 400°F and bake for 10 minutes, or until golden and crisp.

Spiced Chicken Naans

Serves 2

4 tablespoons plain yogurt

1 tablespoon jalfrezi curry paste

2 tablespoons lemon juice

2 skinless, boneless chicken breasts, each cut into 8 pieces

1 small red onion, thinly sliced

1 small green pepper, cored, seeded, and thinly sliced

4 tablespoons passata

2 garlic and cilantro naan breads

5 oz mozzarella cheese, drained and sliced

- Mix together the yogurt, jalfrezi paste, and lemon juice. Add the chicken pieces and stir to coat. Place the chicken on a foil-lined broiler pan with the onion and pepper slices and cook under a preheated hot broiler for 5–8 minutes, turning occasionally, until the chicken is cooked and beginning to char at the edges and the onion and pepper slices have softened slightly.

- Spread the passata onto the naan breads, and arrange the chicken, onion, pepper, and mozzarella slices on top. Line the broiler pan with a clean piece of foil. Place the naan breads on the foil, reduce the broiler to medium heat, and cook the naan "pizzas" for 5–8 minutes, or until the cheese has melted and the topping is hot.

Spiced Chicken Salad with Poppadoms Mix together 4 tablespoons mayonnaise with 1 teaspoon mild curry paste, 2 tablespoons mango chutney, and 1 tablespoon roughly chopped fresh cilantro leaves. Stir in 7 oz ready-cooked chicken tikka and half a diced apple. Serve with diced cucumber and ready-to-eat poppadoms.

Hot Spiced Chicken and Mango Chutney Chapati Wraps Coat 2 chopped skinless, boneless chicken breasts with a mixture of 4 tablespoons plain yogurt, 1 tablespoon jalfrezi paste, and 2 tablespoons lemon juice. Cook under a hot broiler for 5–8 minutes, turning occasionally, until cooked and beginning to char at the edges. Place on 2 warmed chapatis with 1 small, thinly sliced red onion, some fresh cilantro leaves, and 2 tablespoons mango chutney. Roll up the chapatis and serve.

Mozzarella Chicken Melts

Serves 4

1 tablespoon sun-dried tomato
   pesto
2 tablespoons olive oil
2 chicken breasts, halved
   horizontally
4 thick slices of sourdough bread
2 tablespoons tapenade
1¼ cups cherry tomatoes, halved
small handful of basil leaves,
   roughly torn
5 oz mozzarella cheese, drained
   and sliced
green salad, to serve

- Mix together the tomato pesto and 1 tablespoon olive oil and spread over both sides of the chicken pieces.

- Heat the remaining olive oil in a skillet over medium heat, add the chicken, and cook for 8–10 minutes, turning once until the chicken is cooked through.

- Toast the sourdough bread. Spread the tapenade on one side of each slice and arrange the cooked chicken, cherry tomatoes, basil, and mozzarella on top. Place on a broiler pan and cook under a preheated broiler until the tomatoes are hot and the mozzarella has melted. Serve with a simple green salad.

Italian Chicken Toasties

Butter 8 slices of crusty bread. Spread the unbuttered side of 4 of the slices with 2 tablespoons tapenade. Arrange 7 oz sliced cooked chicken, 2 sliced tomatoes, a handful of basil leaves, and 5 oz sliced mozzarella cheese on top. Place the remaining bread on top, butter-side up. Cook in a sandwich press for about 5 minutes, or until golden and crisp, or in a skillet over medium heat, turning once, until the bread is crisp and the filling hot.

Baked Chicken

Coat 2 halved chicken breasts in a mixture of 1 tablespoon sun-dried tomato paste and 1 tablespoon olive oil. Season and place in a baking dish with 1¼ cups halved cherry tomatoes, 1 thinly sliced zucchini, and a small handful of torn basil leaves. Arrange 5 oz sliced mozzarella on top and drizzle with a little olive oil. |Cook in a preheated oven at 400°F for 25 minutes, or until the chicken is cooked and the vegetables are tender. Serve with crusty bread.

Smoked Chicken Bruschetta

Serves 4

½ ciabatta loaf, cut into ½ inch
  slices
2 tablespoons olive oil
1 garlic clove, crushed
2 scallions, finely chopped
4 ripe tomatoes, finely chopped
1 tablespoon chopped fresh basil
1 tablespoon balsamic vinegar
1 smoked cooked chicken breast,
  torn into small pieces
salt and pepper

- Place the bread slices on a cookie sheet. Mix together the oil and garlic and brush over the bread. Bake in a preheated oven at 350°F for 10 minutes, or until crisp.

- Meanwhile, mix together the scallions, tomatoes, basil, and balsamic vinegar together in a bowl. Season with salt and pepper, then add the chicken pieces and toss to coat.

- Spoon the tomato mixture onto the toasted slices of bread to serve.

**Smoked Chicken
Ciabatta**

Combine the tomato and scallion as above and spread onto toasted slices of ciabatta. Top with sliced smoked chicken and basil leaves to serve.

**Smoked Chicken
and Tomato Tarts**

Cut a puff pastry sheet into 4 rectangles. Use a sharp knife to score a line ½ inch in around the edges. Transfer to a baking pan, lightly brush with beaten egg, and bake in a preheated oven at 400°F for 15 minutes, or until well risen and golden. Meanwhile mix together 2 finely diced

scallions, 4 diced tomatoes, 1 tablespoon chopped basil, and 1 tablespoon balsamic vinegar. Season with salt and pepper. Remove the pastry from the oven and push the center of each tart down. Set one-quarter of the tomato mixture into each indentation. Place slices of smoked chicken on top, garnish with basil leaves, and serve.

Lemon, Mint, and Chicken Skewers

Serves 4

scant ¾ cup Greek-style yogurt

finely grated zest and juice of
1 lemon

2 tablespoons chopped mint

2 tablespoons olive oil

4 skinless, boneless chicken
breasts, each cut into 8 pieces

salt and pepper

To serve

4 pita breads, warmed

cucumber, sliced

radish, sliced

- Whisk together the yogurt, lemon zest and juice, mint, and olive oil. Add the chicken pieces and stir well to coat.

- Thread the chicken onto 4 skewers and place on a foil-lined broiler pan. Cook under a preheated hot broiler for about 10 minutes, turning occasionally, until the chicken is cooked and slightly charred at the edges. Slide the chicken off of the skewers and serve stuffed in warm pita bread along with slices of cucumber and radish.

10 Lemon Chicken Pitas

Make a lemon mint dressing by whisking together 2 tablespoons mayonnaise, 2 tablespoons Greek-style yogurt, 1 teaspoon finely grated lemon zest, and 1 tablespoon chopped mint. Warm 4 pita breads and stuff with sliced cooked chicken, sliced cucumber, and sliced radish, drizzled with dressing.

30 Baked Lemon Chicken with Garlic Roast Tomatoes

Coat 4 skinless, boneless chicken breasts, each cut in half widthwise, in a mixture of a scant ¾ cup Greek-style yogurt, the finely grated zest and juice of 1 lemon, 2 tablespoons chopped mint, and 2 tablespoons olive oil. Place the coated chicken on a foil-lined baking pan along with 4 halved tomatoes. Scatter with 1 minced garlic clove, drizzle with olive oil, and season with salt and pepper. Bake in a preheated oven at 425°F for 20 minutes, turning once, until the chicken is cooked and the tomatoes are soft. Serve with quick-bake french fries.

QuickCook

Midweek Meals

Recipes listed by cooking time

30

20

Chicken Pesto Pasta

Serves 4

12 oz penne or other pasta shapes

large handful of basil leaves

3 tablespoons toasted pine nuts, plus extra to serve

¼ cup freshly grated Parmesan cheese, plus extra to serve

1 garlic clove, peeled

3 tablespoons olive oil

6 oz cooked chicken

handful of pitted black olives

salt and pepper

- Cook the penne in lightly salted boiling water for 10 minutes or until just tender.

- Meanwhile, make the pesto. Put the basil, pine nuts, Parmesan, garlic, and olive oil in a small food processor or blender and process until almost smooth.

- Drain the cooked penne and return to the pan. Add the pesto, chicken, and olives. Season with salt and pepper and gently heat through. Scatter with the extra pine nuts and Parmesan to serve.

Chicken Pasta Salad with Pesto Dressing Cook 250 g quick-cook pasta bow ties in lightly salted boiling water for 5 minutes or until al dente. Drain, rinse under cold running water, and drain again. Toss with a mixture of 1 tablespoon pesto, 1 tablespoon olive oil, and 1 teaspoon balsamic vinegar. Add 7 oz cooked chopped chicken, 8 halved cherry tomatoes, 2 cups baby spinach, and a handful of toasted pine nuts. Lightly toss together and serve immediately.

Crispy Pesto Breadcrumbed Chicken Cut 4 skinless, boneless chicken breasts in half horizontally. Smear each piece with ready-made pesto. Pour 1 cup ready-made lemon and black pepper flavored bread crumbs onto a plate. Roll the chicken in it to coat then set on a foil-lined baking pan. Drizzle generously with olive oil. Bake in a preheated oven at 400°F for 25 minutes, or until the chicken is cooked and the bread crumbs are crisp. Serve with oven-baked french fries and broccoli.

Moroccan Fruity Chicken Stew

Serves 4

1 tablespoon olive oil

1 large red onion, cut in large chunks

1 onion, cut into large chunks

¾ lb cubed chicken

1 teaspoon ground cumin

1 teaspoon paprika

1 teaspoon ground coriander

½ teaspoon ground cinnamon

½ teaspoon ground ginger

generous ½ cup dried prunes

½ cup dried apricots

15½ oz can chickpeas

2½ cups rich chicken stock

1 tablespoon cornstarch, blended with 2 tablespoons water

4 tablespoons chopped cilantro

- Heat the oil in a large, heavy saucepan and cook the onions and chicken, stirring occasionally, over a moderately high heat for 10 minutes, or until golden in places and soft. Stir in the spices and cook for a further 2 minutes to help the flavors infuse.

- Add the prunes and apricots, chickpeas, and stock and bring to a boil. Cover and cook for 15 minutes until all the ingredients are soft and cooked through.

- Add the blended cornstarch and stir well to thicken slightly, then stir in the fresh cilantro. Serve with couscous, if liked.

---

10 Moroccan Chicken and Bean Soup

Heat 1 tablespoon olive oil in a saucepan, add 1 thinly sliced red onion and ½ lb thinly sliced chicken breast. Cook for 3–4 minutes. Add 1 teaspoon each ground cumin and ground coriander, and ½ teaspoon ground cinnamon and cook for 30 seconds. Pour in 2½ cups chicken stock and a 15½ oz can drained chickpeas. Boil, reduce the heat, and add a scant ¼ cup roughly diced dried prunes. Cook for 4 minutes more until piping hot. Process in a blender for a smooth soup, if liked.

20 Moroccan Baked Potatoes

Cook 4 baking potatoes in the microwave for about 15 minutes, or until soft. Meanwhile, heat 1 tablespoon olive oil in a large, heavy saucepan over high heat. Add 1 sliced onion and 2 thinly sliced chicken breasts, each weighing about 5 oz, and cook for 5 minutes. Add ½ teaspoon each of ground cumin, ground coriander, ground paprika, and ground cinnamon and cook for a further 1 minute. Add ¾ cup diced mixed ready-to-eat dried prunes and apricots to the pan with ¾ cup chicken stock and bring to a boil. Reduce the heat and simmer gently for 5 minutes. Add a 15 oz can mixed beans in tomato sauce and heat for a further 3–4 minutes, stirring occasionally, until piping hot and the chicken is thoroughly cooked. Split open the potates and divide the sauce among the openings to serve.

Warm Chicken Liver, Butternut Squash, and Bacon Salad

Serves 4

4 tablespoons olive oil

1½ lb butternut squash, peeled, if liked, seeded and cut into small chunks

¾ lb chicken livers, thawed if frozen, and drained

6 slices bacon, roughly chopped

1 cup walnut halves

4½ cups watercress

pepper

balsamic vinegar, to serve

- Heat 3 tablespoons of the oil in a large, heavy skillet or wok over medium-high heat and cook the butternut squash, stirring occasionally, for 15–20 minutes until softened and cooked through.

- Meanwhile, in a separate heavy skillet heat the remaining oil over high heat and cook the chicken livers and bacon, stirring almost continually to prevent it from sticking, for 10 minutes, or until golden and cooked through. Add the walnuts and cook for a further minute to warm through.

- Toss the chicken livers, bacon, walnuts, and butternut squash together in a large bowl, season with pepper, and set aside to cool for 3–4 minutes.

- Just before serving add the watercress to the bowl and toss with the other ingredients. Arrange the salad on 4 warmed serving plates and drizzle with balsamic vinegar.

Chicken Liver, Bacon, and Pine Nut Salad Heat 2 tablespoons olive oil in a large, heavy skillet over high heat and add ½ lb drained chicken livers together with 6 slices bacon, diced, and fry for 5 minutes. Meanwhile, put 3 tablespoons pine nuts into a small skillet and cook over low heat for 3–4 minutes until lightly toasted. Place 4½ cups watercress in a large salad bowl. Add the warm chicken livers and bacon and the toasted pine nuts, and toss together. Dress with balsamic vinegar and olive oil.

Chicken Liver and Bacon Salad with Peppers and Onions Core and seed 1 red and 1 orange pepper and cut into chunks. Heat 2 tablespoons olive oil in a large, heavy skillet over medium heat. Add the peppers along with 1 thinly sliced red onion and fry for 4–5 minutes, or until softened and golden in places. Remove from the pan with a slotted spoon, then add ½ lb drained chicken livers and 6 slices bacon, diced. Cook over high heat for 4 minutes, or until cooked through. Add 1 cup walnut halves and cook for a further 2 minutes. Transfer to a large bowl along with 5 cups baby spinach leaves and toss well. Drizzle with balsamic vinegar to serve.

Coronation Chicken

Serves 4

¾ cup mayonnaise
1–2 teaspoons medium curry
   paste
1 tablespoon lemon juice
1 tablespoon chopped fresh
   cilantro
¾ lb cooked chicken, chopped
¾ cup seedless grapes, halved
2 tablespoons raisins
salt and pepper

To serve

watercress
crusty bread

- Mix together the mayonnaise, curry paste, lemon juice, and half the cilantro. Season with salt and pepper.
- Lightly stir in the chicken, grapes, and raisins. Scatter with the remaining cilantro and serve with watercress and crusty bread.

2 Coronation Chicken and Three-Grain Salad Cook 4 oz three-grain risotto mix (rice, barley, and spelt) in lightly salted boiling water for 10 minutes or until just tender. Drain, rinse under cold running water, and drain again. Lightly stir the risotto into the coronation chicken mixture. Scatter with toasted flaked almonds to serve.

3 Coronation Chicken and Potato Salad Cook ¾ lb new potatoes in lightly salted boiling water for 10–15 minutes, or until tender. Drain and cut in half. Leave to cool, then mix with ¾ lb chopped cooked chicken, ¾ cup mayonnaise, 1–2 teaspoons medium curry paste, 1 tablespoon lemon juice, 1 tablespoon chopped fresh cilantro, and a small bunch of scallions, chopped.

Pan-Fried Chicken with Garlicky Mashed Beans

Serves 4

8 small boneless, skinless chicken thighs

1 tablespoon sunflower oil

1 tablespoon wholegrain mustard

¾ cup apple juice or dry apple cider

2 × 15½ oz cans lima beans, rinsed and drained

4 tablespoons garlic-flavored oil

2 tablespoons roughly chopped flat-leaf parsley

salt and pepper

- Flatten the chicken thighs and season well with salt and pepper. Heat the oil in a skillet over high heat, add the chicken thighs, and cook for 5 minutes, turning once, until golden.

- Stir the mustard and apple juice or apple cider into the skillet, reduce the heat, and simmer for 10 minutes, or until the sauce is reduced and slightly thickened.

- Meanwhile, heat the lima beans in a pan with the garlic oil and 2 tablespoons water for a few minutes until hot. Mash with a potato masher, season with salt and pepper, and stir in the flat-leaf parsley. Serve with the chicken and the pan juices.

Mustard Chicken with Kale and Lima Beans Fry ¾ lb chicken tenders in 1 tablespoon sunflower oil for 3 minutes. Stir in 1 tablespoon wholegrain mustard, 7 oz washed Scots kale, and a 15½ oz can rinsed and drained lima beans. Cover and cook for 5 minutes, or until the kale is tender. Stir in 1 scant cup crème fraîche, season with salt and pepper, heat through, and serve.

Stuffed Chicken Thighs with Mashed Beans Flatten 8 small boneless, skinless chicken thighs. Spread one side of them with 6 oz soft blue cheese, roll the thighs up, and wrap them each in a slice of bacon. Hold each in place with toothpicks. Fry in 1 tablespoon sunflower oil over high heat for 5 minutes, turning occasionally, until browned. Add 1 tablespoon wholegrain mustard and ¾ cup apple juice or dry apple cider and simmer for 10–15 minutes, or until the chicken is cooked through. Serve with mashed lima beans as above.

Chicken and Piquante Pepper Tortilla

Serves 4

2 tablespoons olive oil

1 large red onion, sliced

½ lb chicken thigh meat, thinly sliced

5 tablespoons chopped parsley

1 tablespoon chopped rosemary leaves

14 oz jar piquante peppers, drained

5 eggs, beaten

salt and pepper

- Heat the oil in a large, heavy skillet, about 10 inches across, over medium-high heat. Add the onion and chicken and cook for 8–10 minutes, or until soft and cooked through. Add the parsley, rosemary, and peppers and stir and cook for a further 2 minutes.

- Beat the eggs with plenty of salt and pepper then pour them over the chicken and onions and cook gently over low heat for 5 minutes, or until the base is set. Place under a preheated hot broiler to cook the top for 4–5 minutes, or until just set. Cut into wedges and serve with a simple salad and crusty bread, if liked.

---

1 **Fluffy Chicken and Pepper Wok Omelet** Heat 2 tablespoons olive oil in a large wok over medium heat. Add 1 large, finely sliced red onion and fry for 3 minutes. Then add 3½ oz diced cooked chicken, 2 oz drained and roughly diced piquante peppers, and 2 tablespoons chopped frozen parsley. Pour in 6 beaten eggs and cook over high heat until the base is beginning to set. Keep flipping the omelet in the pan until both sides are just set. Scatter with some freshly grated Parmesan cheese, if liked, slice into 4 pieces, and serve.

2 **Chicken and Piquante Pepper Omelet** Heat 1 tablespoon olive oil in a large, heavy skillet over medium-high heat. Add 1 large sliced red onion and ½ lb chopped chicken thigh meat. Fry, stirring occasionally, for 8–10 minutes, or until golden and cooked. Add 10 oz drained piquante peppers from a jar and add to the skillet with 1 tablespoon chopped rosemary. Season generously and cook for a further 1 minute to heat through. Heat another 1 tablespoon olive oil in a heavy 8 inch skillet over low heat and cook half the egg mixture as above for 3–4 minutes. Remove from the skillet with a spatula or slotted turner and keep warm while heating another 1 tablespoon olive oil and cooking the remaining egg to make a second thin omelet. Fill each with half the chicken mixture, fold the omelet over to enclose the filling, and cut each in half to serve.

Chicken, Chorizo, and Broccoli Pasta

Serves 4

8 oz rigatoni or other pasta shapes

2 cups broccoli florets

2 tablespoons olive oil

2 skinless, boneless chicken breasts, sliced

6 oz chorizo, thickly sliced

1 scant cup crème fraîche

4 teaspoons chopped parsley

salt and pepper

freshly grated Parmesan cheese, to serve

- Cook the rigatoni in lightly salted boiling water for 10 minutes, or until just tender, adding the broccoli for the final 5 minutes of the cooking time.

- Meanwhile, heat the oil in a skillet over medium heat, add the chicken and chorizo, and fry for 5–8 minutes, or until the chicken is cooked through. Stir in the crème fraîche and heat through, then add the parsley. Add a little water if the sauce becomes too thick.

- Stir in the pasta and broccoli and stir well. Season with salt and pepper and serve with plenty of freshly grated Parmesan cheese.

10 Chicken and Tomato Ravioli

Cook 11½ oz ready-made chilled spinach-and-ricotta-filled ravioli in lightly salted boiling water for 3 minutes or according to the instructions on the package. Drain, tip back into the pan, add 6 oz chopped cooked chicken, 3 oz chopped cooked chorizo, and 13½ oz pouch or can of ready-made tomato and basil sauce. Heat through and serve with freshly grated Parmesan cheese scattered on top.

30 Chicken, Chorizo, and Leek Lasagne

Fry 2 chopped skinless, boneless chicken breasts, 6 oz chopped chorizo, and 1 sliced leek in 2 tablespoons olive oil over high heat for 5 minutes. Stir in a 13½ oz pouch or can of ready-made tomato pasta sauce and heat through. Place alternating sheets of fresh lasagne and the sauce mixture in an ovenproof dish. Pour 11½ oz ready-made fresh cheese sauce on top and bake in a preheated oven at 400°F for 20 minutes, or until golden and bubbling. Serve with broccoli.

Thai Red Curry with Chicken Meatballs

Serves 4

1 lb ground chicken
1 tablespoon lemon grass paste
1 teaspoon ginger paste
7 tablespoons chopped fresh cilantro
1 small red bird's-eye chile, minced
1 tablespoon vegetable oil
2 tablespoons red Thai curry paste
13½ fl oz can coconut milk
salt and pepper
boiled rice, to serve (optional)

- Put the ground chicken in a large bowl with the lemon grass paste, ginger paste, 3 tablespoons of the chopped fresh cilantro, and the minced red chile. Season with salt and pepper and mix well with a fork to blend the spices into the chicken. Shape the mixture into 32 walnut-size balls.

- Add the oil to a large, heavy skillet over high heat. Add the meatballs and fry for 8–10 minutes, in batches if necessary, until golden in places, lightly shaking the pan to turn the meatballs. Blend the curry paste into the coconut milk and pour over the meatballs. Bring to a boil, reduce the heat, and simmer for 5 minutes. Stir in the remaining fresh cilantro and serve with boiled rice, if liked.

Thai Burgers

Put ¾ lb ground chicken in a bowl with 1 tablespoon Thai curry paste and 3 tablespoons chopped fresh cilantro. Shape the flavored chicken into 4 patties and flatten as much as possible without breaking the patties. Add 1 tablespoon vegetable oil to a large, heavy skillet on high heat. Fry the patties for 2–3 minutes on each side, or until golden and cooked through. Serve in hamburger buns with salad.

Thai Chicken Stir-Fry

Prepare 1 lb ground chicken as above, blending it with the lemon grass, ginger paste, fresh cilantro, and chile. Place 1 tablespoon vegetable oil in a large wok or skillet over high heat. Add the ground chicken and fry, stirring occasionally, for 7–8 minutes until golden and crisp in places. Add 4 cups sugar snap peas, 1 diced red pepper, and 1 diced orange pepper. Stir-fry for a further 4 minutes, add 1 scant cup coconut milk and 2 teaspoons red Thai curry paste. Cook, stirring constantly, for 2 minutes until piping hot. Spoon into warmed bowls to serve.

Chicken Satay

Serves 4

12 ready-made chicken satay skewers

2 × 8 oz packages ready-cooked Thai rice

4 tablespoons mayonnaise

2 tablespoons crunchy peanut butter

1 teaspoon Thai red curry paste

2 scallions, sliced

- Reheat the chicken satay skewers in a microwave or in a hot skillet for 2–3 minutes.

- Reheat the rice in a microwave or saucepan according to the instructions on the package.

- Mix together the mayonnaise, peanut butter, and Thai curry paste and pour into a small serving bowl.

- Serve the chicken skewers with the rice and sauce, with the scallions scattered on top.

Chicken Satay and Noodle Salad

Soak 7 oz rice vermicelli noodles in boiling water for a few minutes until softened, then drain. Meanwhile, stir-fry 3 sliced skinless, boneless chicken breasts in 1 tablespoon peanut oil for 5 minutes. Add 1 tablespoon dark soy sauce and 1 tablespoon sweet chili sauce and simmer for 1 minute. Mix the noodles and chicken with 4 cups baby spinach leaves, and 2 cups snow peas. Whisk together 2 tablespoons crunchy peanut butter, 1 tablespoon sweet chili sauce, 2 tablespoons lemon juice and 1 tablespoon peanut oil. Toss with the salad and serve.

Chicken Satay Skewers

Cut 4 skinless, boneless chicken breasts into strips and coat in a mixture of 1 tablespoon dark soy sauce, 1 teaspoon dark brown sugar, 1 teaspoon lemon grass paste, and 1 teaspoon Thai red curry paste. Leave to marinate for 10 minutes. Thread the chicken onto skewers, concertina style, and place them on a foil-lined broiler pan. Cook under a preheated hot broiler for 5 minutes, or until cooked through. Make a peanut dipping sauce by warming 2 tablespoons crunchy peanut butter with 1 teaspoon Thai red curry paste and 4 tablespoons coconut cream. Serve the chicken skewers with the peanut sauce on the side and a crisp salad.

Basil, Ricotta, and Sun-Dried Tomato Chicken

Serves 4

4 chicken breasts, skin on
1 scant cup ricotta cheese
small handful of basil leaves
¾ cup sun-dried tomatoes
2 tablespoons olive oil
salt and pepper

To serve

spinach
new potatoes

- Cut a slit along the length of each chicken breast to make a large pocket. Divide the ricotta among the pockets, stuffing it well inside. Then insert some basil leaves and sun-dried tomatoes. Press the chicken together firmly to close the pockets and season with salt and pepper.

- Heat the oil in a large skillet, add the chicken breasts, skin-side down, and fry for 15 minutes, turning once, until golden and the chicken is cooked through. Serve with spinach and new potatoes and the juices from the pan.

Mediterranean Omelet (serves 2)

Beat together 6 eggs with 2 tablespoons water. Season with salt and pepper. Heat 2 tablespoons butter in a large skillet until foaming, pour in the beaten eggs, and cook for 1 minute. Use a wooden spatula to draw the set egg into the center of the pan allowing the uncooked egg to run to the sides. When golden brown underneath and softly set on top dot with spoonfuls of ½ cup ricotta cheese, a few basil leaves, ¼ lb thinly sliced cooked chicken, and ¾ cup diced sun-dried tomatoes. Fold the omelet in half and slide onto a large plate to serve.

Baked Basil and Ricotta Chicken with Roasted Vegetables

Cut 4 chicken breasts (with skin on) down the side to form pockets. Fill with 1 scant cup ricotta cheese, a few basil leaves, and ¾ cup diced sun-dried tomatoes. Press together firmly and place on baking pan with 2 sliced zucchini, 1 cored and seeded red pepper, 3 unpeeled garlic cloves, and ¾ lb new potatoes (halved if large). Season, drizzle with olive oil, and add a few sprigs of rosemary. Roast in a preheated oven at 400°F for 25 minutes, or until the chicken is cooked and the vegetables are tender.

30 Chicken, Feta, and Spinach Pasties

Serves 4

6 oz frozen spinach, thawed and
   well drained
6 oz cooked chicken breast, torn
   into pieces
½ teaspoon ground nutmeg
2 tablespoons softened butter
3 tablespoons toasted pine nuts
2 oz feta cheese, crumbled
8 sheets of filo pastry
salt and pepper
salad, to serve

- Put the spinach in a bowl with the chicken, nutmeg, and half the softened butter and mix together. Season with plenty of pepper and a little salt. Add the pine nuts and feta and mix to combine.

- Place the sheets of filo pastry on a cutting board and fold in half widthwise. Spoon the chicken mixture evenly onto the center of each piece and fold one side over to cover the filling. Fold the other side over that, then fold the opposite sides, one under and one over the pasty, to form a square. Place on a cookie sheet and repeat with the remaining 7 sheets. Melt the remaining butter and brush it lightly over the top surface of each pasty.

- Bake in a preheated oven at 400°F for 15 minutes, or until golden and cooked through. Serve with a simple salad.

1 Chicken, Feta, and Spinach Stir-Fry

Heat 2 tablespoons oil in a large wok or skillet and cook 2 thinly sliced chicken breasts for 5 minutes. Add 10 oz ready-washed spinach and ½ teaspoon grated nutmeg. Toss and stir for 2 minutes until wilted. Season generously with salt and pepper. Crumble 7 oz feta cheese and scatter it, along with 3 tablespoons toasted pine nuts, onto the stir-fry. Serve with plenty of crusty bread.

2 Chicken and Spinach Tarts

Cut 4 sheets of filo pastry in half. Fold each piece in half widthwise and place in a 4-hole Yorkshire pudding pan or deep muffin pan, ruffling the pastry so that it fits into the hole. Lightly brush with 1 tablespoon melted butter and bake in a preheated oven at 400°F for 5–6 minutes, or until golden and crisp. Meanwhile, put 1 tablespoon butter in a skillet and add ¼ lb torn cooked chicken breast, 8 oz thawed frozen spinach, and ½ teaspoon nutmeg. Heat, stirring, for 5 minutes until piping hot. Crumble 2 oz feta cheese and stir it, along with 3 tablespoons toasted pine nuts, into the mixture. Remove from the heat. Divide the hot filling between the 4 hot pastry cases and serve with a simple salad.

Thai Red Curry Soup

Serves 4

1 tablespoon sunflower oil

2 skinless, boneless chicken
   breasts, cut into strips

¾ lb butternut squash, peeled and
   cut into small pieces

1 red pepper, cored, seeded, and
   cut into small pieces

1 tablespoon Thai red curry paste

13½ fl oz can reduced-fat
   coconut milk

2½ cups chicken stock

6 oz green beans, halved

small handful of fresh cilantro
   leaves, roughly chopped

- Heat the oil in a large saucepan, add the chicken, butternut squash, and red pepper and fry over high heat for 5 minutes.

- Add the curry paste, fry for 1 minute, then stir in the coconut milk, stock, and green beans. Bring to a boil, reduce the heat, cover, and simmer for 10 minutes until the chicken and vegetables are cooked. Stir in the fresh cilantro and serve.

---

1 Chicken, Butternut Squash, and Vermicelli Soup Heat 2½ cups ready-made chilled spiced butternut squash soup in a saucepan. Stir in ¼ lb chopped cooked chicken and 3 oz vermicelli rice noodles. Simmer for 5 minutes, or until the noodles are soft, and serve.

3 Spiced Thai Chicken and Rice Fry 8 small chicken thighs (with skin on) in 1 tablespoon vegetable oil over high heat for 5 minutes, turning once. Add 2¾ cups diced butternut squash, 1 diced red pepper, and ¼ lb halved green beans and cook for a further 5 minutes. Stir in 1 tablespoon Thai red curry paste, 1½ cups long-grain rice, 13½ fl oz can coconut milk, and 2 cups chicken stock. Simmer for 15–20 minutes, or until the liquid is absorbed and the rice is tender. Scatter with fresh cilantro leaves to serve.

Potato, Chicken, Bacon, and Thyme Gratin

Serves 4

1 lb potatoes (not peeled), thinly sliced

2 tablespoons olive oil

1 onion, thinly sliced

2 chicken breasts, weighing about 5 oz each, thinly sliced

6 slices Canadian bacon, thinly sliced

3 tablespoons thyme leaves, plus a few sprigs to garnish (optional)

1¼ cups heavy cream

5 tablespoons freshly grated Parmesan cheese

salt and pepper

- Cook the potatoes in a large saucepan of lightly salted boiling water for 10 minutes, or until just tender, then drain.

- Meanwhile, heat the oil in a large, heavy skillet over high heat and add the onion, chicken, and bacon. Cook, stirring occasionally, for 5 minutes, or until cooked through.

- Layer the potatoes in a large, shallow gratin dish with the chicken, bacon, onion, and a scattering of thyme leaves, finishing with a layer of potatoes. Season the cream with a little salt and pepper and pour over the potatoes. Scatter with the Parmesan and cook under a preheated hot broiler for 4–5 minutes, or until the topping is golden and the cream bubbling. Scatter with some thyme sprigs, if using, and serve with a simple green salad.

---

10 Chicken, Bacon, and Thyme Stir-Fry

Heat 2 tablespoons olive oil in a large, heavy skillet over medium heat. Add 3 thinly sliced chicken breasts, each weighing about 5 oz, and 6 slices of bacon, diced, and fry for 8 minutes, stirring occasionally. Add 1 tablespoon thyme leaves and 1¾ cups crème fraîche. Season generously and serve with instant mashed potatoes scattered with freshly grated Parmesan cheese.

20 Creamy Chicken and Bacon Pie

Slice 2 large potatoes and cook in a saucepan of lightly salted boiling water for 10 minutes or until tender, then drain. Meanwhile, heat 1 tablespoon olive oil in a large, heavy wok or skillet over medium heat and cook ¾ lb diced chicken and 6 slices of bacon, diced, for 10 minutes, or until golden. Add 1 tablespoon thyme leaves and 2 × 10½ oz cans condensed cream of chicken soup and heat for 2–3 minutes until hot. Transfer to a large, shallow gratin dish and place the drained potato slices on top. Lightly brush the tops of the potatoes with 1 tablespoon olive oil and scatter with 3 tablespoons freshly grated Parmesan cheese. Place under a hot broiler and cook for 2–3 minutes, or until golden, then serve.

30 Crispy Salt and Pepper Chicken Thighs

Serves 4

8 chicken thighs, each weighing about ¼ lb
scant ½ cup all-purpose flour
½ teaspoon salt flakes
1 teaspoon black pepper
1 tablespoon olive oil
3 teaspoons thyme leaves and sprigs, to garnish

- Tighten the flesh and skin around the bone of each chicken thigh and pierce with a toothpick so the skin remains taut.

- Put the flour in a large bowl and stir in half the salt and pepper. Add the thighs and toss until lightly coated.

- Heat the oil in a large, heavy skillet over medium heat and cook the chicken, skin-side up, for 5 minutes, turning once, until golden.

- Transfer the chicken to a roasting pan, skin-side up, and season with the remaining salt and pepper. Cook in a preheated oven at 400°F for 20–25 minutes, or until the chicken is golden and cooked through; when the chicken is pierced the juices should run clear.

- Scatter with the thyme leaves and sprigs to garnish and serve with steamed green vegetables or a crisp salad.

---

1 Salt and Pepper Chicken Tenders
Put a scant ½ cup all-purpose flour in a bowl and season with 1 teaspoon black pepper and a little salt. Toss 1 lb chicken tenders in the seasoned flour until lightly coated. Heat 4 tablespoons olive oil in a large, heavy skillet or wok over high heat. Add the chicken and cook for 7–8 minutes until golden, crisp in places, and cooked through. Remove from the pan with a slotted spoon and drain on paper towels before serving hot with mustard mayonnaise and a salad, if liked.

2 Salt and Pepper Chicken Thighs with an Herb Coating Cut 8 chicken thighs, each weighing about ¼ lb, from the bone, and then into 2 large pieces. Put a scant ½ cup all-purpose flour in a large bowl with 1 teaspoon black pepper, ½ teaspoon salt, and 4 tablespoons chopped mixed herbs, such as parsley, thyme, and rosemary. Toss the chicken in the seasoned flour to coat. Place 4 tablespoons olive oil in a large, heavy skillet over high heat and cook the chicken, turning once, for 10 minutes. Reduce the heat and cook for a further 5 minutes.

Paprika Chicken with Peppers

Serves 4

1 tablespoon sunflower oil
¾ lb chicken tenders
1 teaspoon garlic paste
1 tablespoon paprika
6 oz frozen sliced mixed peppers
1 tablespoon tomato paste
¾ cup sour cream
salt and pepper

- Heat the oil in large skillet over high heat, add the chicken, and stir-fry for 5 minutes. Add the garlic paste, paprika, peppers, and tomato paste and cook, stirring, for 3 minutes.

- Stir in the sour cream, season with salt and pepper, and heat through. Serve with freshly cooked tagliatelle.

Paprika Chicken and Gnocchi Gratin

Prepare the Paprika Chicken with Peppers as above. When it is ready, stir in 13 oz gnocchi, which have been cooked in lightly salted boiling water for 5 minutes and drained. Pour into a heatproof dish, scatter with ½ cup grated cheddar cheese, and cook under a preheated broiler for 5 minutes, or until the cheese is hot and bubbling.

Paprika Chicken Casserole

Fry 4 skinless, boneless chicken breasts on medium heat in 1 tablespoon sunflower oil for 5 minutes, turning once, until golden. Add 1 diced onion and 1 diced green pepper and fry for 3 minutes. Stir in 1 tablespoon paprika, 1 tablespoon tomato paste, and a 13½ oz can diced tomatoes. Simmer for 15 minutes, season with salt and pepper, ⌡and stir in ¾ cup sour cream. Serve with mashed potatoes.

Oriental Ground Chicken

Serves 4

1½ cups long-grain rice
1 tablespoon sunflower oil
1 lb ground chicken
6 scallions, diced
1 red chile, seeded and thinly
    sliced
2 tablespoons black bean sauce
1 tablespoon light soy sauce
¾ cup chicken stock
1 teaspoon cornstarch, mixed to a
    smooth paste with a little water
salt and pepper

- Cook the rice in lightly salted boiling water for 10 minutes until tender, then drain.

- Meanwhile, heat the oil in a wok or large skillet over high heat. Add the ground chicken and stir-fry for 5 minutes until it forms clumps.

- Add the scallions and chile and cook for 2 minutes. Stir in the black bean sauce, soy sauce, and stock. Simmer, stirring occasionally, for 5 minutes. Season with salt and pepper and pour in the cornstarch paste. Cook, stirring, until thickened slightly. Serve with the cooked rice.

Ground Chicken in Black Bean Sauce with Shrimp Crackers

Stir-fry 1 lb ground chicken in 1 tablespoon sunflower oil over high heat for 5 minutes. Add a scant ½ cup ready-made black bean stir-fry sauce and cook for 3 minutes. Scatter with thinly sliced scallions and serve with shrimp crackers.

Oriental Chicken Meatballs

Mix 1 lb ground chicken with 1 crushed garlic clove and season with salt and pepper. Roll the mixture into 24 small balls and fry in 2 tablespoons sunflower oil over medium heat for 8–10 minutes, or until golden and cooked. Remove from the pan. Fry 3 cored, seeded, and diced mixed color peppers and 1 onion, cut into wedges, for 5 minutes.

Drain an 8½ oz can pineapple chunks in natural juice, reserving the juice. Add the pineapple chunks to the pan with the meatballs. Stir in 3 tablespoons hoisin sauce, 1 tablespoon light soy sauce, and 5 tablespoons of the reserved pineapple juice. Stir in 1 teaspoon cornstarch mixed to a smooth paste with a little water and bring to a boil, stirring, until slightly thickened. Serve with rice.

CHI-MIDW-ZUK

Chicken and Rustic Fries

Serves 4

4 small baking potatoes, cut into chunky wedges

6 tablespoons olive oil

1 teaspoon salt flakes

4 boneless chicken breasts, skin on, each weighing about 5 oz

2 tablespoons all-purpose flour

½ teaspoon mustard powder

1 teaspoon black pepper

2 tablespoons chopped parsley

salt

- Coat the potato wedges in 4 tablespoons of the oil and toss with the salt flakes. Transfer to a baking pan and roast in a preheated oven at 400°F for 20–25 minutes, or until golden in places.

- Meanwhile, cut each chicken breast in half across its width to make 2 thin chicken breasts. Put the flour in a large bowl with the mustard powder, pepper, and parsley. Season with a little salt. Mix well, add the chicken pieces, and toss well to coat lightly in the seasoned flour.

- Heat the remaining oil in a large skillet over medium-high heat and cook the chicken, turning once, for 8–10 minutes, or until golden and cooked through. Serve the chicken with the rustic fries along with mayonnaise flavored with mustard, and an arugula salad, if liked.

---

10 Seasoned Chicken Strips with Herby Mashed Potatoes Toss 12 chicken tenders with 2 tablespoons all-purpose flour mixed with 1 teaspoon chicken seasoning. Heat 3 tablespoons olive oil in a large, heavy skillet over high heat. Add the chicken. Cook for 5 minutes until golden and cooked through. Serve with instant mashed potatoes with chopped parsley for color and 1 tablespoon crème fraîche per serving stirred through.

20 Pan-Fried Chicken and Herby Cubed Potatoes Chop 3 potatoes into small cubes. Heat 3 tablespoons olive oil in a large, heavy skillet over medium-high heat and cook the potatoes, stirring occasionally, for 12–15 minutes, or until golden and soft. Meanwhile, put 12 chicken tenders in a bowl with 2 tablespoons all-purpose flour, ½ teaspoon black pepper, and ½ teaspoon mustard powder. Toss well until the chicken is lightly coated. Heat a further 3 tablespoons olive oil in a separate skillet over high heat, add the chicken, and cook for 8–12 minutes, or until golden and cooked through. Toss 3 tablespoons chopped parsley into the potatoes and serve with the pan-fried chicken.

Chicken Curry in a Hurry

Serves 4

2 tablespoons sunflower oil

4 skinless, boneless chicken thighs, chopped

2 sweet potatoes, peeled and cubed

3 tablespoons balti curry paste

13½ oz can diced tomatoes

1¼ cups chicken stock

1 scant cup frozen peas

small handful of fresh cilantro leaves, roughly chopped

naan bread, to serve

- Heat the oil in a large skillet over high heat, add the chicken and sweet potatoes, and fry, stirring, for 5 minutes.

- Add the curry paste, tomatoes, and stock to the skillet, bring to a boil, reduce the heat, cover, and simmer for 10 minutes. Stir in the peas and cook for a further 5 minutes. Stir in the fresh cilantro and serve with warm naan bread.

Curried Chicken Naans

Mix together 3 tablespoons mayonnaise, 2 teaspoons curry paste, and 1 teaspoon tomato paste. Stir in 7 oz chopped cooked chicken, 2 sliced celery sticks, and ¼ diced cucumber. Warm 4 small naan breads, place Little Gem lettuce leaves and the curried chicken mixture on top, and serve.

Creamy Chicken Curry

Fry 1 sliced onion in 1 tablespoon sunflower oil for 5 minutes, or until softened. Add 4 chopped skinless, boneless chicken breasts and fry for 10 minutes. Stir in 1 cup diced no-need-to-soak apricots. Mix together 2 tablespoons medium curry paste, 1¼ cups plain yogurt, and ¾ cup heavy cream. Pour into the pan, bring to a boil, and simmer for 5 minutes. Scatter with fresh cilantro leaves and serve with rice.

 # Chicken with Potatoes, Blue Cheese, and Tomatoes

Serves 4

2 lb potatoes, roughly cubed

3 tablespoons vegetable oil

2 chicken breasts, each weighing about 5 oz, thinly sliced

2 teaspoons Cajun spice

½ lb baby plum tomatoes

10 oz fresh spinach, washed and drained

4 oz Danish blue cheese, crumbled

- Cook the potatoes in a large pan of lightly salted boiling water for 5 minutes. Drain well and set aside.

- Meanwhile, heat the oil in a large wok or skillet over high heat. Add the chicken and fry for 5 minutes, or until golden and cooked. Remove from the pan with a slotted spoon and set aside. Add the drained potatoes to the pan and cook over high heat for 10 minutes, or until golden and softened.

- Return the chicken to the pan along with the Cajun spice and toss well to coat. Add the tomatoes and spinach and sauté for 5 minutes, until the tomatoes have softened and the spinach has wilted.

- Crumble the cheese into the pan and remove from the heat. Toss lightly to allow the cheese to soften slightly, then spoon onto warmed serving plates to serve.

---

1 Chicken, Spinach, and Blue Cheese

Croquettes Mix 3½ oz instant mashed potatoes with boiling water or according to the instructions on the package. Add 1 roughly chopped chicken breast and a handful of roughly chopped fresh spinach. Stir in 2 oz crumbled blue cheese. Shape into 4 croquettes and flatten slightly. Put 3 tablespoons vegetable oil in a large, heavy skillet over high heat. Add the croquettes and fry for 2 minutes on each side until golden. Serve with a green salad.

2 Chicken, Spinach, and Blue Cheese

Rösti Cut 1 lb potatoes in half and cook in a large pan of salted boiling water for 5 minutes. Drain, grate, and put in a bowl with a large handful of shredded spinach, 2 oz finely chopped cooked chicken, and 2 oz blue cheese, crumbled. Mix together well and form into 4 patties. Put 3 tablespoons vegetable oil in a large, heavy skillet over medium heat. Add the rösti and fry for 2–3 minutes on each side, or until golden and crisp in places. Drain on paper towels and serve hot with a green salad.

Chicken and Corn Chowder

Serves 4

14¾ oz can cream style sweet corn

2 cups milk

6 oz cooked chicken, torn into pieces

¾ cup frozen whole kernel sweet corn

2 scallions, chopped

2 teaspoons cornstarch

salt and pepper

crusty bread, to serve

- Place the cream style sweet corn in a large saucepan with the milk and heat, stirring.

- Add the chicken, whole sweet corn kernels, and scallions and season with salt and pepper. Simmer for 5 minutes, stirring occasionally.

- Blend the cornstarch with 1 tablespoon water, pour into the soup, and stir to thicken. Ladle into bowls and serve with crusty bread.

Chicken and Corn Fritters

Mix together ¾ cup all-purpose flour, 1 teaspoon baking powder, a little salt and pepper, 1 egg, and ¾ cup milk to make a smooth batter. Stir in 1 cup sweet corn kernels and 6 oz chopped cooked chicken. Fry large spoonfuls of the mixture in 1 tablespoon sunflower oil for 2 minutes on each side until golden. Serve with crisp slices of bacon and ketchup.

Chicken, Bacon, and Corn Chowder

Dice 2 slices of bacon and fry with 1 diced onion and 2 diced medium potatoes in 2 tablespoons of butter for 5 minutes. Pour in |2 cups milk and simmer for |10 minutes. Stir in ¾ cup frozen whole kernel sweet corn and 6 oz chopped cooked chicken. Season with salt and pepper and heat through. Scatter with chopped fresh parsley to serve.

Chicken Thighs with Spinach, Lemon, and Ricotta Filling

Serves 4

8 skinless, boneless chicken
thighs, each weighing
about ¼ lb
1 tablespoon olive oil
7 oz fresh spinach, washed and
drained
1 teaspoon ground nutmeg
finely grated zest of 1 lemon
4 oz ricotta cheese
salt and pepper

- Unroll the chicken thighs on a board and season well with little salt and plenty of black pepper.

- Put the oil in a pan over medium heat. Add the spinach and cook for 2 minutes, stirring continually until wilted. Remove from the heat and drain well, pressing the leaves into a sieve to remove any excess liquid. Roughly chop the spinach. Place in a bowl and add the nutmeg and lemon zest. Season with pepper. Stir in the ricotta to combine.

- Put spoonfuls of the mixture in the center of the chicken thighs and roll up so filling does not fall out, holding the chicken together loosely with toothpicks.

- Transfer to a roasting pan and bake in a preheated oven at 400°F for 15 minutes, or until cooked. Serve hot with a simple salad and warm crusty bread.

---

1 **Chicken with Ricotta, Sun-Dried Tomatoes, and Pine Nuts**
Cut 4 chicken breasts, each weighing about ¼ lb, almost in half widthwise and open up. Heat 1 tablespoon olive oil in a skillet and fry the chicken, turning once, for 7–8 minutes, or until cooked through. In a small pan mix together 4 oz ricotta cheese, ½ teaspoon nutmeg, the finely grated zest of 1 lemon, and 2 tablespoons toasted pine nuts. Stir in 5 sun-dried tomatoes, diced, and 2 tablespoons milk and gently heat. Spoon the mixture over the chicken and serve.

2 **Chicken with Ricotta, Sun-Dried Tomatoes, and Basil** Mix together 4 oz ricotta cheese, 8 roughly diced sun-dried tomatoes, and 3 tablespoons chopped basil. Cut 4 chicken breasts, each weighing about ¼ lb, in half across their width and fill each with spoonfuls of the ricotta mixture. Hold the edges together with toothpicks. Heat 2 tablespoons olive oil in a large, heavy skillet over medium-high heat. Add the chicken and cook for 5 minutes on each side. Cover with a lid and cook for a further 3 minutes.

Serve hot with a simple watercress salad and warm crusty bread, if liked.

Chicken Chili Pasta

Serves 4

1 tablespoon sunflower oil

1 lb ground chicken

1 garlic clove, crushed

1 teaspoon chili powder

½ teaspoon dried red pepper flakes

2 cups passata

1 tablespoon sun-dried tomato pesto

¾ lb spaghetti

salt and pepper

freshly grated Parmesan cheese, to serve

- Place the oil in a large skillet over high heat, add the ground chicken, and fry for 5 minutes, breaking up any clumps.

- Add the garlic, chili powder, dried red pepper flakes, passata, and pesto and stir. Season with salt and pepper, bring to a boil, then reduce the heat and simmer for 10 minutes.

- Meanwhile, cook the spaghetti in lightly salted boiling water for 8–10 minutes, or until al dente. Drain and toss with the chicken chili sauce. Serve with plenty of freshly grated Parmesan cheese.

Chili Chicken with Tortilla Chips

Heat a 14 oz jar of ready-made tomato and chili pasta sauce in a saucepan. Add 1 cup rinsed and drained canned red kidney beans and 6 oz chopped cooked chicken and heat through. Serve with sour cream and tortilla chips.

Baked Chili Chicken

Cut several slashes across the top of 4 chicken breasts (with skin on) and place them in a foil-lined roasting pan. Whisk together 5 tablespoons balsamic vinegar, 2 tablespoons lemon juice, 4 tablespoons olive oil, and 1 diced red chile and pour it over the chicken breasts. Bake in a preheated oven at 400°F for 25 minutes with 1 lb frozen roast potatoes on another baking pan on a separate shelf until the chicken is cooked through and the potatoes are crunchy on the outside. Serve with peas.

# Chicken, Broccoli, and Cheese Bake

Serves 4

2 tablespoons olive oil

3 chicken breasts, each weighing about ¼ lb, thinly sliced

10 oz broccoli florets

1 lb pouch or jar of ready-made fresh cheese sauce

1 teaspoon grated nutmeg

¼ ciabatta loaf, torn into bite-size pieces

4 tablespoons olive oil

½ teaspoon salt flakes

½ teaspoon black pepper

2 tablespoons fresh chopped parsley

4 tablespoons freshly grated Parmesan cheese

- Preheat the oven to 400°F. Place the oil in a large, heavy skillet or wok over medium heat. Add the chicken and fry for 5 minutes, stirring occasionally, or until golden and cooked.

- Meanwhile, put the broccoli in a pan of lightly salted boiling water and cook for 5 minutes, or until just tender. Drain and toss with the cooked chicken. Stir in the cheese sauce, add the nutmeg, and toss well to coat. Cook, stirring occasionally, for 2–3 minutes until hot. Transfer to a shallow heatproof gratin dish, or 4 individual gratin dishes.

- Meanwhile, put the bread in a large bowl with the oil and toss well. Add the salt, pepper, and herbs and toss again.

- Distribute the bread pieces over the chicken mixture and scatter evenly with the Parmesan. Bake for 15 minutes, or until golden and bubbling. Serve with a simple salad, if liked.

Chicken, Broccoli, and Cheese Soup

Put 8 oz small broccoli florets in 1¼ cups boiling water, cover with a tight-fitting lid, and cook for 5 minutes. Add 15 oz pouch or jar of ready-made fresh cheese sauce, ¼ lb cooked chicken, and ½ teaspoon grated nutmeg. Bring to a boil then transfer to a food processor or blender and process until smooth.

Chicken, Broccoli, and Cheese Gratin

Make the chicken, broccoli, sauce, and nutmeg mixture as above and heat until piping hot. Spoon the mixture into 4 individual gratin dishes. Mix together 1 cup bread crumbs and 2 tablespoons freshly grated Parmesan cheese and scatter evenly over each gratin dish. Place under a preheated hot broiler and cook for 5 minutes, or until piping hot and golden in places. Serve with a simple salad.

30 Smoky Cannellini Bean Stew with Sausages and Chicken

Serves 4

1 tablespoon olive oil
4 good-quality pork sausages
10 oz chicken, roughly diced
1 red onion, sliced
1 red pepper, cored, seeded, and
   cut into strips
3½ oz chorizo sausage, sliced
2 teaspoons smoked paprika
2 × 15 oz cans cannellini beans,
   rinsed and drained
14½ oz can diced tomatoes
2½ cups chicken stock
1 tablespoon cornstarch
4 tablespoons chopped parsley

- Heat the oil in a large, heavy skillet over medium heat and add the sausages. Fry them, turning occasionally, for 10 minutes, or until golden and cooked through. Remove from the pan with a slotted spoon and transfer to a plate lined with paper towels. Set aside to cool and drain.

- Add the chicken to the pan and stir-fry for 3 minutes. Add the onion and pepper and cook for 3 minutes more before adding the chorizo and cooking for a further 2 minutes. Stir in the smoked paprika. Add the beans, tomatoes, and stock and bring to a boil. Cut the sausages into thick chunks and add to the pan. Reduce the heat, cover, and simmer for 10 minutes.

- Blend the cornstarch with 2 tablespoons water and add to the pan with the parsley. Stir well until thickened slightly.

- Ladle the stew into warm bowls and serve with crusty bread to mop up the juices.

---

10 Smoky Chicken and Beans on Toast

Heat 1 tablespoon olive oil in a skillet over high heat and add 2 thinly sliced chicken breasts, each weighing about 5 oz. Cook for 3–4 minutes then add 1 teaspoon smoked paprika, a 10 oz jar drained roasted peppers, a 15 oz can cannellini beans, and a 14½ oz can diced tomatoes. Bring to a boil and cook for 3 minutes, or until piping hot. Serve on thick slices of toast.

20 Smoky Chicken and Bean Stew

Place 1 tablespoon olive oil in a large saucepan over medium heat. Add 1 sliced onion and 2 thinly sliced chicken breasts, each weighing about 5 oz, and cook for 3–4 minutes. Add 1 thinly sliced red pepper and 1 thinly sliced zucchini and cook for 2–3 minutes. Stir in 2 teaspoons smoked paprika, and then add 2 × 15 oz cans cannellini beans and 2½ cups chicken stock and bring to a boil.

Reduce the heat and simmer for 5 minutes before adding 4 teaspoons cornstarch blended with 2 tablespoons water. Stir well to thicken. Serve with crusty bread.

QuickCook
Family
Favorites

Recipes listed by cooking time

Roasted Chicken Thighs with Roots and Honey

Serves 4

4 chicken thighs

4 small parsnips, each quartered lengthwise

4 large carrots, each quartered lengthwise

3 tablespoons olive oil

3 tablespoons clear honey

pepper

4 tablespoons chopped parsley, to garnish

- Put the chicken thighs in a roasting pan with the parsnips and carrots. Drizzle with the olive oil and shake the vegetables and chicken to coat in the oil. Season generously with pepper and roast in a preheated oven at 425°F for 20–25 minutes, or until golden, drizzling everything with the honey for the final 3 minutes of cooking.

- Scatter with the parsley and serve with instant mashed potatoes and a green vegetable, if liked.

1 Sticky Chicken and Carrot Stir-Fry with Honey and Thyme

Heat 2 tablespoons olive oil over high heat. Add ¾ lb diced chicken meat and cook for 2 minutes to seal. Add 2 large thinly sliced carrots and stir-fry for 6–7 minutes, or until the chicken and carrots are cooked through. Drizzle with 4 tablespoons clear honey and 1 tablespoon thyme leaves and toss to coat. Serve with instant mashed potatoes or quick-cooking rice.

2 Honeyed Chicken Breasts with Baby Carrots, Parsnips, and Thyme

Place 2 tablespoons olive oil in a large, heavy skillet over high heat. Add 4 chicken breasts, each weighing 3–4 oz, and cook for 2 minutes on each side to seal. Add 6 oz baby carrots and 2 roughly diced peeled parsnips. Continue to cook over high heat, turning all the ingredients occasionally, for 10 minutes or until golden and cooked through. Season generously with pepper then stir through 2 tablespoons clear honey. Garnish with 1 tablespoon chopped thyme leaves and serve.

CHI-FAMI-VIW

Chicken Biryani

Serves 4

1¼ cups basmati rice

2 tablespoons oil

1 large onion, thinly sliced

10 oz diced chicken

1 bay leaf

3 cardamom pods

1 teaspoon turmeric

4 tablespoons curry paste

¾ cup chicken stock

generous ½ cup raisins

4 tablespoons plain yogurt

scant ¾ cup toasted flaked
  almonds

4 tablespoons chopped fresh
  cilantro, to garnish

- Cook the rice in a large saucepan of lightly salted boiling water for 15–20 minutes, or until tender.

- Meanwhile, put the oil into a large, heavy skillet over medium-high heat. Add the onion and chicken and cook for 5–8 minutes, or until golden, adding the bay leaf, cardamom, and turmeric for the final minute of cooking.

- Add the curry paste and stir-fry for 1 minute, then pour in the stock. Bring to a boil, add the raisins and yogurt, and cook gently for 10 minutes, until the stock has reduced by half.

- Drain the cooked rice, add to the pan with the chicken, and toss and cook for 2–3 minutes. Scatter with flaked almonds and garnish with chopped fresh cilantro to serve.

1 Simple Fruity Chicken Biryani

Cook 1¼ cups quick-cooking rice and set aside. Put 1 tablespoon oil in a heavy skillet over high heat and add ½ lb diced chicken. Cook for 8 minutes, or until golden. Add 2 tablespoons curry paste, a generous ½ cup raisins, and 4 tablespoons flaked almonds. Mix well. Add the cooked rice and toss everything together before garnishing with fresh cilantro to serve.

2 Green Chicken Biryani

Place 1 cup easy-cook long-grain rice in a large saucepan of lightly salted boiling water and cook for 10–12 minutes, or until tender. Put 2 tablespoons oil in a large, heavy skillet over medium heat. Add ½ lb diced chicken along with 8 tablespoons chopped fresh cilantro and cook for 5–8 minutes, or until golden in places. Add 3 tablespoons curry paste and stir-fry for 3 minutes before adding a 13½ oz can of spinach. Reduce the heat and cook for 3–4 minutes, or until piping hot. Drain the rice well and add to the pan with the chicken and spinach, toss well over the heat, and serve.

CHI-FAMI-VAO

Tomato, Chicken, Pepper, and Olive Tuscan-Style Tarts

Serves 4

12 oz rolled puff pastry sheet

2 tomatoes, sliced

5 oz spicy tomato-flavored
   chicken slices

8 small pieces of roasted pepper,
   drained, from a jar

1 tablespoon thyme leaves

¾ cup kalamata olives, drained

1 tablespoon olive oil

salt and pepper

green salad, to serve

- Unroll the puff pastry sheet, cut it into 4 x 5 inch disks, and arrange on a large baking pan, spaced well apart. Prick the pastry all over with a fork.

- Arrange the tomato slices randomly on top of each disk, dividing them evenly between the pastry disks and keeping a ½ inch border around the edge. Scatter evenly with the chicken slices, peppers, thyme, and olives, then drizzle with the olive oil and season with salt and pepper.

- Bake at the top of a preheated oven at 425°F for 12–15 minutes, or until the pastry is puffed up and golden and the topping is soft. Serve the tarts with a simple green salad.

Savory Chicken and Pepper Croustades Cut 2 foccacia rolls in half. Drizzle each side with 1 tablespoon olive oil and place under a preheated broiler. Cook for 2 minutes, or until warm. Set aside wrapped in foil to keep warm. Place 5 oz sliced chicken breast in a pan with 10 oz drained, sliced, roasted red peppers from a jar, and a generous ¼ cup kalamata olives. Warm through over gentle heat, stirring occasionally, for 4–5 minutes, or until hot. Stir through 3 tablespoons chopped parsley and serve spooned over the warm toasted foccacia halves.

Tuscan Tart with Artichokes and Lemon Unroll a 12 oz sheet of puff pastry onto a large baking pan. Drain a 12 oz jar of artichokes in oil, place in a bowl, and mix with the finely grated zest of 1 lemon and 4 tablespoons chopped parsley. Scatter this onto the pastry sheet. Toss 5 oz cooked spicy tomato chicken slices with 1 tablespoon olive oil and scatter over the top of the artichokes with 1 diced tomato and ¾ cup drained kalamata olives. Bake in a preheated oven at 425°F for 25 minutes, or until the pastry is well puffed up and golden.

Chicken and Boston Beans

Serves 4

1 tablespoon olive oil

2 chicken breasts, each weighing about 5 oz, thinly sliced

1 onion, thinly sliced

1 tablespoon molasses

1 tablespoon wholegrain mustard

1 tablespoon soft dark brown sugar

14½ oz can diced tomatoes

16 oz can baked beans

3 tablespoons chopped parsley

pepper

whole-wheat toast, to serve

- Place the oil in a heavy, medium-sized saucepan over medium heat. Add the chicken and onion and fry for 3–4 minutes.

- Stir in the molasses, mustard, sugar, and tomatoes, bring to a boil, and simmer for 2 minutes before adding the beans. Then stir in the parsley and heat through for 1 minute.

- Spoon the mixture onto 4 thick, freshly toasted slices of whole-wheat bread, season with pepper, and serve.

---

2 Paprika Boston Baked Beans with Chicken and Bacon

Heat 2 tablespoons olive oil in a large skillet and cook 1 thinly sliced onion, 2 thinly sliced chicken breasts, and 4 slices of bacon, diced, for 5 minutes, or until golden, soft, and cooked through. Add 1 teaspoon paprika, 1 tablespoon molasses, 1 tablespoon wholegrain mustard and 2 tablespoons soft dark brown sugar and stir well. Stir in 14½ oz can diced tomatoes and 2 × 15 oz cans cannellini beans. Bring to a boil, cover, and simmer for 10 minutes, removing the lid for the final 2 minutes. Stir through 2 tablespoons chopped parsley and serve.

3 Cannellini Boston Bean Gratin

Heat 2 tablespoons olive oil in a large, heavy skillet over medium-high heat. Add 1 large thinly sliced onion and 2 thinly sliced chicken breasts, each weighing about 5 oz, and cook for 5 minutes. Stir in 2 tablespoons molasses, 1 tablespoon wholegrain mustard, and 1 tablespoon soft dark brown sugar, 14½ oz can diced tomatoes, and 2 × 15 oz cans cannellini beans. Bring to a boil and simmer for 8–10 minutes, or until the mixture has thickened. Transfer to a large, shallow gratin dish. In a bowl mix together 1½ cups whole-wheat bread crumbs, ½ cup freshly grated Parmesan cheese, and 2 tablespoons chopped parsley. Scatter the mixture evenly over the beans and right up to the edges of the dish. Place under a preheated medium-hot broiler and cook for 3–4 minutes, or until the top is golden and the cheese has melted. Serve with a simple salad and bread to mop up the juices.

Spicy Chicken Wings with Avocado Salsa

Serves 4

2 tablespoons oil

4 tablespoons tomato ketchup

3 tablespoons sweet chili sauce

½ teaspoon dried red pepper flakes

1 tablespoon clear honey

½ teaspoons ground black pepper

1½ lb chicken wings

For the avocado salsa

1 avocado, diced

½ cup cherry plum tomatoes, quartered

2 tablespoons fresh chopped cilantro

finely grated zest and juice of 1 lime

1 teaspoon olive oil

ground black pepper

- Mix together the oil, ketchup, chili sauce, dried red pepper flakes, honey, and pepper in a large mixing bowl. Add the chicken wings and stir well to coat them in the mixture.

- Arrange the wings in a single layer on the rack of a foil-lined broiler pan. Place under a preheated hot broiler for and cook for 10 minutes on one side, before turning the wings and cooking them for 5–7 minutes on the other side, until the chicken is cooked through.

- Meanwhile, make the avocado salsa by mixing together all the salsa ingredients in a small bowl and seasoning generously with pepper. Serve the chicken piping hot with the salsa separately and crusty bread to mop up the juices, if liked.

Spicy Chicken Cubes with Guacamole Mix together the ketchup, chili sauce, dried red pepper flakes, honey, and pepper as above in a mixing bowl. Add ¾ lb chicken breast, cubed, and ¾ cup cherry tomatoes. Toss well to coat. Place on a rack in a foil-lined broiler pan and set under a preheated hot broiler. Cook, turning once, for 7–8 minutes, or until lightly charred in places and cooked through. Serve with spoonfuls of ready-made guacamole.

Roasted Chicken Wings with Barbecue Sauce and Griddled Peppers Mix together 4 tablespoons tomato ketchup, 4 tablespoons soft brown sugar, and 1 tablespoon red wine vinegar. Add 3 tablespoons clear honey and mix well. Add 1½ lb small chicken wings and toss in the mixture to coat. Arrange the wings in a single layer in a roasting pan and cook in a preheated oven at 425°F for 25 minutes, or until cooked through and lightly charred in places. Meanwhile, cut 1 red and 1 orange pepper into large chunks. Heat 1 tablespoon olive oil on a ridged griddle pan and cook the peppers for 5–10 minutes, or until lightly charred and softened. Toss with the barbecued chicken and serve with rice, if liked, and with any remaining juices from the pan spooned over the chicken.

Chicken, Bacon, and Mushroom Pie

Serves 4

3 tablespoons olive oil

¾ lb diced chicken

6 slices bacon, diced

3½ CUPS crimini mushrooms, halved

3 oz butter

scant ¼ cup all-purpose flour

1¼ cups milk

2 tablespoons wholegrain mustard

4 tablespoons chopped parsley

2 tablespoons thyme leaves

4 oz pouch instant mashed potato mix

2 tablespoons freshly grated Parmesan cheese

salt and pepper

- Heat 1 tablespoon of the oil in a large skillet over high heat and cook the chicken and bacon for 8–10 minutes, or until golden. Meanwhile, in a separate pan, heat the remaining oil over high heat and cook the mushrooms, stirring, for 5 minutes, or until golden and soft. Mix the cooked mushrooms with the bacon and chicken.

- In a medium-sized saucepan melt 2 oz of the butter, stir in the flour and cook for 1 minute. Remove from the heat and add the milk, a little at a time, stirring between each addition until blended. Return to the heat and stir until boiled and thickened. Stir in the mustard and season, then set aside.

- Add the parsley and half the thyme to the chicken and bacon. Stir in the sauce and transfer to a shallow gratin dish.

- Make the mashed potatoes according to the instructions on the package. Add the remaining butter and thyme and beat well to fluff up. Spoon onto the chicken and bacon mixture and scatter with the Parmesan. Cook under the preheated broiler for 3–4 minutes, or until golden and bubbling.

10 **Creamy Chicken and Bacon Pan-Fry with Spinach** Heat 1 tablespoon olive oil in a large, heavy skillet over high heat. Add ½ lb diced chicken and ½ lb diced bacon and cook for 7–8 minutes, or until golden. Add 10 oz washed spinach and stir-fry with the chicken for 2 minutes before adding ¾ cup crème fraîche with 1 tablespoon wholegrain mustard. Heat for 1 minute over high heat until piping hot. Serve with warm crusty bread.

 20 **Creamy Chicken, Mushroom, and Bacon Pan-Fry with Herby Mashed Potatoes** Heat 2 tablespoons olive oil in a large skillet over high heat. Add ¾ lb diced chicken with ½ lb diced bacon and cook for 8–10 minutes, or until golden and cooked through. In a separate wok or heavy skillet heat 2 tablespoons olive oil over medium heat. Add ½ lb halved crimini mushrooms and cook for 8–10 minutes, or until golden and soft. Add the chicken to the mushrooms and add 1¾ cups crème fraîche, 1 tablespoon thyme leaves, and 1 tablespoon wholegrain mustard. Make mashed potatoes from a 4 oz pouch according to the instructions on the package then mix with 1 tablespoon thyme leaves. Ladle the chicken mixture onto the potates and serve hot.

Flattened Chicken with Prosciutto and Gruyère

Serves 4

4 chicken breasts, each weighing about ¼ lb
1 egg, beaten
1½ cups fresh white bread crumbs
4 tablespoons olive oil
4 slices of Gruyère cheese
4 slices of prosciutto
sage leaves, to garnish

- Put the chicken breasts between 2 sheets of oiled plastic wrap and beat with a rolling pin until almost doubled in size and set aside. Place the beaten egg on one plate and the bread crumbs on another. Lightly coat each chicken breast in egg and then in bread crumbs. Set aside.

- Put the oil in a large, heavy skillet over medium heat. (You may need to use 2 skillets so you can cook all the chicken at the same time.) Cook the chicken for 4 minutes on each side, or until golden and crisp.

- Transfer to 2 baking pans and and set a slice of Gruyère cheese and a slice of prosciutto on top of each. Place under a hot preheated broiler for 2 minutes, then turn off the heat and leave to stand for a further 2 minutes, or until the cheese has melted a little. Serve garnished with sage leaves.

10 Crunchy Chicken Tenders with Warm Gruyère Sauce In a bowl, lightly toss 1 lb chicken tenders in 1 cup fresh white bread crumbs. Put ½ cup olive oil in a large, heavy skillet over medium heat. Add the chicken and cook, turning occasionally, for 7–8 minutes, or until golden and cooked through. Meanwhile, put ½ cup grated Gruyère cheese in a small pan with ¾ cup crème fraîche and 2 teaspoons Dijon mustard. Warm through gently, stirring continuously with a wooden spoon, until the cheese melts. Serve the tenders with the cheese sauce to dip into.

30 Chicken, Gruyère, and Prosciutto Rolls Place 4 chicken breasts, each weighing about ¼ lb, between 2 sheets of oiled plastic wrap and pound until thin and almost doubled in size. Scatter the chicken breasts evenly with ½ cup grated Gruyère cheese. Season generously with plenty of pepper, place a slice of prosciutto on top, and scatter with 2 tablespoons chopped sage. Roll each chicken breast up tightly to form a neat roll and secure with a toothpick. Place 2 tablespoons olive oil in a large, heavy skillet (with a lid) over medium heat. Add the chicken rolls and cook them, turning occasionally, for 10 minutes, or until evenly golden. Cover with the lid for a final 10 minutes of cooking over very low heat. Serve with a simple salad.

CHI-FAMI-CAR

Thick Curried Coconut and Spinach Soup

Serves 4

2 chicken breasts, each weighing about ¼ lb, thinly sliced

1 teaspoon ground coriander

8 oz package quick-cooking rice

2 × 13½ fl oz cans coconut milk

2 tablespoons korma curry paste

1¼ cups chicken stock

6 tablespoons chopped fresh cilantro

10 oz spinach, washed and drained

salt and pepper

naan bread, to serve

· Put the sliced chicken in a large saucepan with the ground coriander, rice, coconut milk, curry paste, and stock and bring to a boil. Cover and simmer for 5 minutes.

· Add the fresh cilantro and spinach and continue to cook, stirring occasionally, for 2–3 minutes more, or until the spinach has wilted. Season generously with salt and pepper, ladle into warmed serving bowls, and serve with warm naan bread.

Hot and Spicy Chicken and Coconut Soup with Okra

Put 2 thinly sliced chicken breasts, each weighing about ¼ lb, in a saucepan with 2 × 13½ fl oz cans coconut milk, 2 tablespoons hot curry paste, 1 thinly sliced bird's-eye chile, 3 tablespoons chopped fresh cilantro, ½ lb roughly diced okra, and 1¼ cups rich chicken stock. Bring to a boil and cook for 15 minutes, or until the mixture is piping hot and the okra is tender. Ladle into warmed serving bowls and serve with warm naan bread.

Thick Lentil, Coconut, and Spinach Soup

Put 2 thinly sliced chicken breasts, each weighing about ¼ lb, in a large, heavy saucepan over medium heat. Add 1 cup red lentils, 2 teaspoons ground coriander, 2 × 13½ fl oz cans coconut milk, 2 tablespoons korma curry paste, 1 bunch of diced scallions, and 1¼ cups chicken stock and bring to a boil. Reduce the heat, cover, and simmer, stirring occasionally, for 20–25 minutes, or until the lentils are tender. Stir in 10 oz spinach in the final 5 minutes of cooking. Serve with warm naan bread.

Chicken, Bacon, Vegetable, and Cheese Layers

Serves 4

4 tablespoons olive oil

2 chicken breasts, each weighing about 5 oz, thinly sliced

6 slices bacon, diced

¾ lb butternut squash, thinly sliced

1 red onion, thinly sliced

4 large tomatoes, sliced

1¼ cups sharp cheddar cheese, grated

4 tablespoons chopped parsley (optional)

- Place the oil in a large, heavy skillet over high heat. Add the chicken breasts and bacon and cook for 3 minutes. Add the thinly sliced butternut squash and onion and continue cooking over high heat for 10 minutes.

- Put a layer of one-half of the sliced tomatoes in the bottom of a shallow, ovenproof dish. Spoon half the chicken and butternut mixture on the top. Scatter evenly with half of the grated cheese. Place another layer of tomatoes on the cheese later then add the remaining chicken and butternut squash, and finally a layer of cheese.

- Place under a broiler preheated to medium and cook for 10–15 minutes, or until golden and bubbling. Garnish with parsley, if liked, and serve with a simple crisp green salad.

---

1 Chicken, Tomato, and Cheese Layers Slice 6 tomatoes and layer the slices in 4 individual shallow gratin dishes with 6 oz cooked chicken slices, 6 tablespoons chopped parsley, and 1¾ cups grated cheddar cheese, finishing off with a layer of cheese. Set the dishes on a broiler pan and cook under a preheated hot broiler for 1 minute, or until golden and softened. Serve with crusty bread.

2 Butternut Squash, Bacon, and Chicken Pan-Fry with Artichokes Put 1 tablespoon olive oil and 2 tablespoons butter in a large, heavy skillet over high heat. Add ½ lb diced chicken and ¼ lb diced bacon and cook for 5 minutes. Meanwhile, peel seed, and thinly slice a ¾ lb butternut squash. Add the slices to the pan and cook, stirring frequently, for a further 10 minutes, or until golden and softened. Drain and quarter a 14 oz can or jar of artichoke hearts, add to the skillet, and cook for 2 minutes, or until hot. Scatter with 6–8 tablespoons chopped flat-leaf parsley and serve on warmed serving plates with freshly grated Parmesan cheese, if liked.

Speedy Roast Chicken with Bacon and Stuffing

Serves 4

4 chicken breasts, each weighing about ¼ lb

2 oz ready-made sage and onion stuffing mix, or enough to make 4 tablespoons stuffing

4 slices bacon

½ lb baby carrots

3 tablespoons olive oil

2 tablespoons chopped parsley

- Put the chicken breasts on a cutting board and slice them lengthwise almost all the way through, leaving a "hinge" at one long end. Make the stuffing mix according to the instructions on the package and use 1 tablespoon of the stuffing to fill each of the breasts. Wrap each tightly with a slice of bacon to hold the stuffing in place.

- Put the chicken and carrots in 1 or 2 roasting pans, drizzle with the oil, and shake gently to coat. Roast in a preheated oven at 400°F for 25 minutes, or until the chicken is golden and cooked through. Scatter with the parsley to garnish before serving.

1 **Simple Chicken and Bacon Pan-Fry with Sage and Onion** Place 3 tablespoons olive oil in a large, heavy skillet over high heat. Add 1 roughly sliced red onion, ¾ lb chicken tenders, and 4 diced slices Canadian bacon and cook, stirring occasionally, for 8–10 minutes, or until golden and soft. Add 1 tablespoon chopped sage leaves and cook for a few more seconds before serving with instant mashed potatoes and chicken gravy, if liked.

2 **Pan-Fried Chicken Wrapped in Bacon with Stuffing Balls** Tightly wrap 4 chicken breasts, each weighing about ¼ lb, in 4 slices of Canadian bacon. Pour 2 tablespoons olive oil into a large, heavy skillet over high heat. Add the chicken, join-side down, and cook for 10 minutes, turning them over halfway through. Meanwhile, make some sage and onion stuffing using 3 oz stuffing mix according to the instructions on the package and shape it into 4 balls.

Add these to the pan, reduce the heat, and cover and simmer for 5 minutes. Garnish with 2 tablespoons chopped flat-leaf parsley before serving.

 Simple Chicken Korma

Serves 4

2 tablespoons oil

1 large onion, roughly diced

1 lb chicken breast, diced

1 teaspoon minced ginger root

1 teaspoon minced garlic

1 teaspoon dried red pepper flakes

1 tablespoon ground coriander

1 teaspoon ground turmeric

1 teaspoon ground garam masala

4 tablespoons ground almonds

1¼ cups plain yogurt

1¼ cups heavy cream

6 tablespoons chopped fresh cilantro

plain rice, to serve

- Place the oil in a large, heavy skillet over medium heat. Add the onion and chicken and cook for 5 minutes, or until softened and golden in places. Add all of the spices, increase the heat to high, and cook for 2–3 minutes, tossing and stirring the mixture until well blended.

- Add the ground almonds and stir to coat the chicken, then stir in the yogurt and cream. Cook, uncovered and stirring occasionally, over low heat for 10 minutes, or until the chicken is cooked and the sauce is well colored and a good consistency, adding a little water if needed. Remove from the heat, stir in the fresh cilantro, and serve with rice, if liked.

Quick Chicken Korma

Place 2 tablespoons oil in a large, heavy skillet over high heat. Add 1 lb diced chicken and cook, stirring occasionally, for 5 minutes, or until golden in places. Add 3 tablespoons korma curry paste and cook for a few seconds before adding 1¼ cups plain yogurt and ½ cup heavy cream. Cook over medium-high heat for 4–5 minutes, or until the sauce has reduced slightly and the chicken is cooked through. Serve with warm naan bread.

 ### Chicken and Potato Korma with Spinach

Cut 6 oz potatoes into chunks and set aside. Place 2 tablespoons oil in a large, heavy saucepan over high heat. Add 1 large diced onion, ¾ lb diced chicken, and the potatoes and cook for 5 minutes, or until golden in places. Add 1 minced garlic clove, 1 teaspoon minced ginger root, and the dried red pepper flakes, ground coriander, turmeric, and garam masala as above. Cook for 2 minutes. Add a generous ½ cup ground almonds and a 13½ fl oz can coconut milk, bring to a boil, reduce the heat, and simmer, stirring occasionally, for 15 minutes. Stir in 1¼ cups plain yogurt and cook for a further 5 minutes, stirring occasionally, until the potatoes are tender and the chicken is cooked. Stir in 13½ oz can of spinach and 4 tablespoons chopped fresh cilantro and heat for 2 minutes more before serving.

Barbecued Squab with Corn and Chile Salsa

Serves 4

2 squab, each cut in half
  lengthwise
finely grated zest and juice of
  1 lime
1 tablespoon Cajun spice mix
2 tablespoons olive oil
8½ oz can whole kernel sweet
  corn
1 red chile, seeded and minced
¼ cucumber, diced
salt and pepper

- Put the squab halves in a large roasting pan and season all over with salt and pepper. Mix together the lime zest and juice, Cajun spice, and 1 tablespoon of the olive oil and brush it all over the squab. Cook on a hot barbecue, turning occasionally, for 25 minutes, or until golden in places and cooked through.

- Meanwhile, put the whole kernel sweet corn in a mixing bowl with the chile, cucumber, and the remaining olive oil. Toss together well and serve with the cooked squab halves.

1 **Spicy Pan-Fried Chicken with Chile and Corn** Place 2 tablespoons olive oil in a large, heavy skillet or wok over high heat. Toss ¾ lb diced chicken with 1 teaspoon Cajun spice and 1 seeded and minced red chile then stir-fry for 5 minutes, or until golden. Add an 8½ oz can drained sweet corn and 2¾ cups sugar snap peas and continue to stir-fry for 3 minutes. Serve in warmed serving bowls with wedges of lime on the side.

2 **Barbecued Chicken Kebabs with Corn and Chile Salsa** Cut 3 skinless, boneless chicken breasts, each weighing about 5 oz, into cubes and place in a bowl with 1 tablespoon olive oil and 2 teaspoons Cajun spice and toss well. Thread the chicken onto 4 bamboo or metal skewers and cook on a hot barbecue for 10–12 minutes, or until lightly charred and cooked through. Meanwhile, make the salsa as above to serve with the kebabs.

Warm Chicken Ciabatta with Salsa and Arugula

Serves 4

1 tablespoon olive oil

2 chicken breasts, each weighing about 5 oz, sliced lengthwise

1 ciabatta loaf, halved

2 ripe tomatoes, roughly diced

1 small red onion, thinly sliced

3 tablespoons chopped parsley

mayonnaise, to taste

mustard, to taste

pepper

arugula, to serve

- Place the oil in a large, heavy skillet over high heat. Toss the chicken breasts with plenty of pepper, add to the skillet, and cook, turning occasionally, for 7–8 minutes, or until golden and cooked through.

- Cut the ciabatta loaf halves into 4 pieces and cook them, cut-side down, on a preheated hot ridged griddle pan for 1–2 minutes, or until lightly toasted.

- Mix together the diced tomatoes, sliced onion, and chopped parsley to make a salsa.

- Arrange the slices of chicken on the 4 ciabatta bottoms and spoon some salsa on top. Spread mayonnaise and mustard on the remaining ciabatta, place on top, and serve with arugula.

---

2 **Hot Tomato, Caramelized Onion, and Chicken Open Sandwich** Heat 4 tablespoons olive oil on medium heat. Add 1 finely sliced red onion. Cook for 15 minutes, or until soft and caramelized. Add 1 tablespoon soft brown sugar for the final 1 minute of cooking. Set aside. Make a salsa by mixing 1 finely diced tomato with 3 tablespoons chopped cilantro, season, and set aside. Heat 1 tablespoon olive oil on medium heat and cook 2 thinly sliced chicken breasts for 4–5 minutes, or until golden. Slice 1 ciabatta loaf in half and spread with mayonnaise then add the hot chicken, onion, salsa, and arugula and serve.

3 **Chicken, Spinach, Tomato, and Red Onion Gratin** Pour 4 tablespoons olive oil into a large, heavy skillet over medium heat. Toss 4 diced chicken breasts, each weighing about 5 oz, with 1 tablespoon pepper, add to the skillet, and cook for 2 minutes. Add 4 roughly diced tomatoes and 1 thinly sliced red onion and cook, stirring occasionally, for 10 minutes, or until softened. Stir in 10 oz fresh spinach and cook for 3 minutes, or until the spinach has wilted. Transfer to a shallow, ovenproof gratin dish. Tear ¼ ciabatta loaf into small, rough pieces and scatter onto the chicken. Then evenly scatter 1 cup grated medium cheddar cheese on top and place under a preheated medium broiler. Cook for 3–4 minutes, or until golden and bubbling.

Chicken, Leek, and Parsley Pies

Serves 4

12 oz ready-made pie pastry
1 egg, beaten
3½ tablespoons butter
¾ lb chicken, diced
2 leeks, finely diced
4 tablespoons chopped parsley
¾ cup white wine
¾ cup heavy cream
2 teaspoons Dijon mustard
salt and pepper

- Roll out the pastry and, using a 6 inch round cookie cutter, cut 4 circles. Place on a large cookie sheet lined with parchment paper. (If you have time, cut leaves from the trimmings and place 4 on top of each circle for decoration.) Glaze with beaten egg and bake in a preheated oven at 400°F for 15 minutes, or until golden and crisp.

- Meanwhile, place the butter in a large, heavy skillet over medium heat. Add the chicken and cook for 10 minutes, or until golden. Add the leeks and cook, stirring occasionally, for a further 5 minutes, or until soft. Stir in the parsley and the wine, increase the heat, and boil to reduce the wine by half.

- Add the cream and mustard and heat through, without boiling, for 1 minute until piping hot. Season generously and ladle the chicken mixture onto 4 warmed serving plates. Place a pastry circle on top and serve with vegetables.

Creamy Chicken and Leeks with Cheesy Mashed Potatoes

Place 2 tablespoons butter in a large, heavy skillet over high heat. Add ½ lb thinly sliced chicken. Cook for 5 minutes or until golden. Add 2 thinly sliced leeks and continue to cook on high heat for 3 minutes, or until softened. Stir in ¾ cup crème fraîche and 1 teaspoon Dijon mustard and heat for a further minute. Heat 1 lb 2 oz ready-made mashed potatoes with cheese and serve the chicken spooned over the potatoes.

Chicken and Leek Pie with Potato Cakes

Heat 2 tablespoons butter in a large, heavy skillet over high heat. Add ¾ lb chicken pieces and cook for 10 minutes. Add 2 finely diced leeks and cook for a further 5 minutes. Whisk 2 teaspoons Dijon mustard with ¾ cup crème fraîche, stir into the skillet, and heat for 1 minute until piping hot. Place 4 potato cakes on a rack in foil-lined broiler pan and place under a preheated medium broiler. Cook for 2–3 minutes, or until piping hot. Ladle the chicken and leek mixture onto 4 warmed serving plates, set a warm potato cake on top of each, and serve.

Whole-Wheat Chicken Tenders with Lemon Mayonnaise

Serves 4

¾ cup all-purpose flour
1¼ lb chicken tenders
2 eggs, beaten
3 cups whole-wheat bread crumbs
2 teaspoons paprika
4 tablespoons chopped parsley
6 tablespoons vegetable oil
crudités: carrot sticks, sliced peppers, and sugar snap peas

For the lemon mayonnaise

¾ cup mayonnaise
finely grated zest and juice of 1 lemon
pepper

- Place the flour in a bowl and add the chicken tenders. Toss well to coat, shaking to remove any excess. Put the beaten eggs in a large bowl. In another bowl, combine the whole-wheat bread crumbs, paprika, and parsley. Dip each chicken slice into the egg and then into the bread crumb mixture.

- Heat the oil in a large, heavy skillet over medium-high heat. Add the chicken in batches, and cook, turning occasionally, for 4–5 minutes, or until golden and crisp on the outside and cooked in the center. Keep the cooked tenders warm while you cook the remainder.

- Meanwhile, make the lemon mayonnaise by mixing the mayonnaise with the lemon zest and juice in a small bowl and seasoning it well with pepper.

- Serve the warm tenders with the lemon mayonnaise and a selection of crudités.

 Pan-Fried Tenders with Lemon Mayo

Cut 3 chicken breasts lengthwise into 5 slices. In a large bowl mix together ¼ cup all-purpose flour, ½ teaspoon pepper, and ½ teaspoon chicken seasoning (optional). Lightly coat the chicken in the flour. Heat 3 tablespoons vegetable oil in a large skillet and cook the chicken, turning frequently, for 7–8 minutes, or until golden and cooked through. Meanwhile, mix ¾ cup mayonnaise with the grated zest and juice of 1 lemon and season well. Serve the hot chicken with lemon mayonnaise for dipping.

Oven-Baked Chicken Parmesan Tenders with Roasted Peppers

Preheat the oven to 400°F. Cut 2 different colored peppers into chunks and toss with 1 tablespoon olive oil. Place in a large roasting pan and roast in the oven while it is heating up. Meanwhile, cut 4 chicken breasts, each weighing about 5 oz, into 4 thick slices. Mix together 1½ cups whole-wheat bread crumbs and ¼ cup freshly grated Parmesan cheese. Press the chicken firmly into the bread crumbs to coat and transfer to the roasting pan with the peppers. Roast for 20 minutes, or until cooked through. Garnish with 2 tablespoons chopped parsley and serve with mayonnaise blended with a little paprika to flavor, if liked.

Chicken Pesto Meatballs in Tomato Sauce with Pasta

Serves 4

¼ lb ground chicken
4 tablespoons pesto
4 tablespoons chopped basil
2 tablespoons olive oil
1 onion, roughly diced
2 × 13½ oz cans diced tomatoes
4 tablespoons tomato paste
salt and pepper
fresh pasta, to serve (optional)

- Put the ground chicken in a mixing bowl with the pesto and basil. Mash together with a fork to blend the pesto and herbs into the ground chicken. Shape the mixture into 24–30 small balls.

- Place 1 tablespoon of the oil in a large, heavy skillet over high heat. Add the chicken balls and cook, shaking the pan occasionally to turn the meatballs, for 15 minutes, or until golden brown and cooked through.

- Meanwhile, put the remaining oil in another skillet over medium-high heat. Add the onion and cook for 3–4 minutes, stirring until softened. Add the diced tomatoes and paste and season generously with salt and pepper. Bring to a boil, reduce the heat, and simmer, uncovered, for 5 minutes or until the sauce has reduced and has thickened slightly.

- Stir the meatballs into the tomato sauce and serve with fresh pasta shapes, if liked.

Chicken Burgers with Pesto Dressing

Shape ¾ lb ground chicken into 4 patties. Place 1 tablespoon olive oil in a large, heavy skillet over medium heat. Add the patties and cook for 3–4 minutes on each side. Season generously with pepper and serve in a whole-wheat hamburger bun with 1 teaspoon pesto spread over each patty and a thick slice of tomato placed on top.

Chicken Meatballs with Pesto Sauce

Shape 1 lb ground chicken into 20 balls. Heat 1 tablespoon olive oil in a large, heavy skillet over high heat and add the chicken balls. Cook for 15 minutes, shaking the pan occasionally to turn the balls, until golden and cooked through. Add 4 tablespoons pesto sauce to the pan, shaking the pan to coat the meatballs in the pesto. Serve on freshly cooked pasta with Parmesan shavings, if liked.

Butter and Lemon Roasted Chicken Thighs

Serves 4

8 boneless, skinless chicken thighs

finely grated zest and juice of 1 lemon

3 tablespoons chopped parsley

2 tablespoons butter

pepper

- Put the chicken thighs in a large mixing bowl with the lemon zest and juice, parsley, and plenty of pepper and mix well to coat the chicken. Roll each of the coated thighs back into shape and secure with a toothpick.

- Put the chicken thighs in a roasting pan, pouring any remaining juices over them, and top each with a small pat of butter. Cook in a preheated oven at 400°F for 20–25 minutes, or until golden and cooked through. Serve with seasonal vegetables.

1 Lemon and Butter Pilaf

Place 1 lb chicken tenders into a bowl with the finely grated zest and juice of 1 lemon and 3 tablespoons chopped parsley. Season generously with salt and pepper. Heat 2 tablespoons butter in a large skillet over high heat. Add the tenders and cook for 6–7 minutes, turning frequently, until golden and cooked through. Toss in 2 x 8 oz packages precooked flavored rice of your choice and cook for a further 2 minutes. Serve immediately.

2 Pan-Fried Thighs with Lemon and Butter

Open out 8 boneless, skinless chicken thighs and cut in half widthwise. Place the chicken pieces in a large mixing bowl with the zest and juice of 1 lemon and 3 tablespoons chopped parsley. Season with salt and pepper and mix well. Put 2 tablespoons butter in a large, heavy skillet over medium heat. Add the chicken and cook for 15 minutes, or until golden and cooked through. Serve with instant mashed potatoes or precooked rice.

Tarragon Chicken Burgers with Spicy Salsa

Serves 4

14½ oz chicken breasts
¾ cup fresh white bread crumbs
6 tablespoons chopped tarragon
1 tablespoon wholegrain mustard
1 tablespoon olive oil
4 whole-wheat hamburger buns,
  sliced open
4 slices of Brie
4 tablespoons ready-made
  spicy salsa

- Put the chicken breasts in a food processor or blender and process until smooth. Add the bread crumbs, tarragon, and mustard and process again. Shape the mixture into 4 balls and flatten them into 4 patties with lightly oiled hands.

- Heat the oil in large, heavy griddle pan or skillet over medium-high heat. Add the burgers and cook, turning once, for 8–10 minutes, or until golden and cooked through.

- Serve the burgers in the hamburger buns with slices of Brie and a spoonful of spicy tomato salsa.

Hot Tarragon Chicken Rolls

Cut 3 chicken breasts, each weighing about ¼ lb, into 4 thin slices widthwise and put them in a bowl with 1 tablespoon olive oil and 2 tablespoons chopped tarragon. Heat 1 tablespoon olive oil in a large, heavy skillet over high heat and add the chicken slices in a single layer. Cook for 5 minutes, turning once, or until golden and cooked through. Serve piled into 4 whole-wheat buns and, while still warm, place a slice of Emmenthal cheese and a spoonful of spicy tomato salsa on top of the chicken, if liked.

Chile and Cilantro Chicken Burgers with Mango and Tomato Salsa

Put ¾ lb chicken breast in a food processor or blender and process until smooth. Add ¾ cup fresh white bread crumbs, ½ small chile, minced, and 3 tablespoons chopped fresh cilantro. Process again to blend. Lightly oil your hands and shape the mixture into 4 balls then flatten them into 4 patties and set aside. Put 1 tablespoon olive oil in a skillet over medium-high heat. Add the burgers and cook for 8–10 minutes, or until golden and cooked through, turning once. Make a salsa. Finely chop ½ ripe mango and place in a bowl with 4 minced scallions, 3 tablespoons chopped fresh cilantro, and ½ small chile, minced. Mix well, season with pepper, and serve spooned onto the burgers in 4 whole-wheat hamburger buns with some arugula on the side.

 # Lentil and Chicken Stew

Serves 4

1 tablespoon olive oil

2 chicken breasts, each weighing about 5 oz, thinly sliced

3 celery sticks, roughly diced

4 roughly diced tomatoes

1¼ cup boiled Puy lentils

13½ oz can diced tomatoes

1 chicken stock cube, crumbled

2 tablespoons chopped parsley

- Place the oil in a medium-sized, heavy skillet over medium heat. Add the chicken and celery and cook for 5 minutes. |Stir in the tomatoes and cook for a further minute.

- Add the lentils, tomatoes, and stock cube together with ¾ cup boiling water. Bring to a boil and keep boiling for 2 minutes, stirring occasionally.

- Stir in the chopped parsley and serve ladled into serving bowls with crusty bread, if liked, to mop up the juices.

 ### Chicken and Paprika Lentil Stew

Put 1 tablespoon oil in a large, heavy saucepan over medium heat. Add diced onion, 2 thinly sliced chicken breasts, each weighing about 5 oz, and cook for 5 minutes. Add 1 teaspoon smoked paprika and 6 diced tomatoes and cook for 1 minute over high heat. Add 1¼ cups boiled Puy lentils and 2½ cups rich chicken stock. Bring to a boil and cook, uncovered, for 10–12 minutes, or until the stew is rich and the stock has reduced slightly. Serve ladled into warmed serving bowls, with warm crusty bread to mop up the juices.

Thick Red Lentil and Chicken Stew

Heat 1 tablespoon olive oil and cook 2 x 5 oz thinly sliced chicken breasts, 1 large thinly sliced onion, and 4 diced celery sticks over medium-high heat for 5 minutes. Add 4 roughly diced tomatoes, 1¼ cups red lentils, 13½ oz can diced tomatoes, and 2½ cups chicken stock. Bring to a boil, reduce the heat, cover, and simmer, stirring occasionally, for 20 minutes or until the lentils are soft and tender. Season with salt and pepper and stir in 6 tablespoons chopped parsley. Serve with warm crusty bread.

Pan-Fried Chicken with Tomato Basil Salsa and Goat Cheese

Serves 4

4 tablespoons olive oil

4 chicken breasts, each weighing about ¼ lb

2 ripe plum tomatoes, finely diced

4 tablespoons chopped basil leaves

1 small red onion, finely diced

1 tablespoon balsamic vinegar

4 thick slices of goat cheese, rind removed

salt and pepper

To serve

salad

crusty bread

- Heat 2 tablespoons olive oil in a large, heavy skillet over medium-high heat. Slice the chicken breasts in half widthwise, almost all the way through, opening the chicken out on its hinge to form a "butterfly." Season all over with a little salt and pepper. Add the chicken to the skillet. Cook for 5 minutes on each side, or until golden and cooked through.

- Meanwhile, make a salsa. Mix together the plum tomatoes, basil, and red onion, the remaining oil, and the balsamic vinegar. Season to taste with salt and pepper.

- Put a slice of goat cheese on each of the chicken breasts, cover the pan with a lid, and cook for a further 1–2 minutes over low heat, or until the cheese melts slightly. Serve the hot chicken on warmed serving plates with the salsa spooned on top along with a simple salad and crusty bread, if liked.

---

1 Chicken, Goat Cheese, and Sun-Blush Tomato Toastie

Heat 2 tablespoons olive oil in a large skillet over high heat. Add 10 oz thinly sliced chicken tenders and fry for 8 minutes, or until golden and cooked through. Meanwhile, toss ½ cup sun-dried tomatoes in oil with 2 tablespoons chopped basil leaves. Lightly toast 4 thick slices of whole-wheat bread. Put the hot chicken on the toast then add a slice of goat cheese on top. Let the cheese melt a little before placing a spoonful of the basil and tomato mixture on top to serve.

3 Chicken, Plum Tomato, Basil, and Goat Cheese Bake

Heat 2 tablespoons olive oil in a large, heavy skillet over high heat. Add 4 chicken breasts, each weighing about 5 oz, and cook for 2 minutes on each side, or until golden. Transfer to a small, shallow gratin dish. Slice 4 large plum tomatoes and place in the dish with the chicken, then scatter with 4 tablespoons chopped basil leaves. Slice 8 oz goat cheese, rind removed, and place on top. Season generously with pepper, drizzle with 2 tablespoons olive oil, and bake in a preheated oven at 400 °F for 15–20 minutes, or until the cheese is golden and the chicken cooked through. Serve with a simple salad and crusty bread.

Fajitas

Serves 4

3 tablespoons olive oil

1 red, 1 green, and 1 orange
   pepper, cored, seeded, and cut
   into chunks

¾ lb diced chicken breasts

2 red onions, cut into thin wedges

1 zucchini, cut into chunks

1 tablespoon Cajun spice

1 tablespoon chopped thyme
   leaves

8 soft flour tortilla wraps

1 avocado, peeled, stoned, and
   roughly diced

finely grated zest and juice of
   ½ lime

salt and pepper

To serve

½ lime cut into wedges

sour cream

- Heat the oil in a large, heavy skillet over high heat. Add the peppers, chicken, and onions and cook, stirring continuously, for 10 minutes, or until golden in places. Add the zucchini and the Cajun spice, toss and stir-fry for 10 minutes, or until the chicken is cooked and the vegetables are softened and lightly charred in places. Stir in the thyme leaves.

- Warm the flour tortillas in the oven or microwave. Meanwhile, to make the guacamole, put the avocado in a bowl and mash well with a fork until smooth but still textured. Season generously with salt and pepper, add the lime zest and juice, and stir well to combine.

- Serve the warm tortillas filled with spoonfuls of the chicken mixture, sour cream, and guacamole, and either rolled or folded, and accompanied by a simple salad, if liked.

Spicy Chicken and Tomato Fajita with Sliced Avocado Heat 2 tablespoons olive oil in a large, heavy skillet over high heat. Add ¾ lb diced chicken and cook for 7 minutes. Add 2 teaspoons Cajun spice and 10 halved cherry tomatoes and stir-fry for 2 minutes before removing from the heat. Serve in warmed tortilla wraps with some avocado slices.

Chicken, Pepper, and Warm Avocado Wraps with Paprika Heat 2 tablespoons olive oil in a large, heavy skillet over high heat. Add ¾ lb diced chicken and 1 large sliced red onion and cook for 7–8 minutes, or until beginning to turn golden. Add 1 large sliced red and 1 sliced orange pepper and cook for 4 minutes. Add 2 tablespoons chopped thyme leaves and 2 teaspoons paprika and continue to cook for 2 minutes. Slice 1 ripe avocado and toss through the mixture. Warm 4 flour tortillas in a oven or microwave and divide the filling among them. Fold to eat, and serve with a simple watercress salad dressed with lime juice.

Sticky Soy-Glazed Drumsticks

Serves 4

8 chicken drumsticks
2 tablespoons clear honey
2 tablespoons olive oil
2 tablespoons dark soy sauce
1 teaspoon tomato paste
1 tablespoon Dijon mustard
chopped parsley, to garnish

- Put the drumsticks on a cutting board and make 4 deep slashes in each one along the thick part of the meat, cutting down to the bone on both sides.

- In a large bowl mix together the honey, oil, soy sauce, tomato paste, and mustard. Toss the drumsticks in the glaze, turning to cover the meat well.

- Transfer the drumsticks to a roasting pan and roast in the top of a preheated oven at 425°F for 20–25 minutes, or until the chicken is cooked through. Garnish with parsley and serve with boiled rice and a salad, if liked.

Soy-Glazed Stir-Fry

Heat 2 tablespoons sunflower oil in a large wok or skillet over high heat. Add ½ lb thinly sliced chicken tenders and stir-fry for 2 minutes. Add 2¾ cups sugar snap peas, 2¾ cups snow peas, and 1 head bok choy, shredded. Stir-fry over high heat for a further 5 minutes. Mix together 2 tablespoons dark soy sauce and 2 tablespoons clear honey, pour into the stir-fry, and toss and cook for a further 1 minute more before serving.

Sticky Chile Soy-Glazed

Chicken Breasts Mix together the honey, oil, soy sauce, tomato paste, and mustard as above to make the glaze and add 1 small minced red chile. Coat 4 chicken breasts, each weighing about ¼ lb, in the glaze. Place 1 tablespoon olive oil in a large, heavy skillet over medium-high heat and cook the chicken for 15 minutes, turning it regularly and reducing the heat a little if the glaze begins to stick to the bottom of the pan. Slice the cooked chicken and serve fanned out on a plate, with boiled rice and salad.

Simple Mango and Coconut Curry with Cilantro

Serves 4

1 tablespoon vegetable oil
1 large onion, diced
1 lb diced chicken meat
1 large, ripe mango, peeled, seeded, and diced
1 teaspoon ground coriander
1 teaspoon ground cumin
2 tablespoons korma curry paste
13½ fl oz coconut milk
1¼ cups rich chicken stock
6 tablespoons chopped fresh cilantro
1 tablespoon cornstarch

- Heat the oil in a large, heavy skillet or wok over high heat. Add the onion and chicken and cook for 5 minutes, or until golden and beginning to soften.

- Add the diced mango, spices, and curry paste and stir for a few seconds before adding the coconut milk and stock. Bring to a boil, then reduce the heat and simmer, uncovered and stirring occasionally, for 10–12 minutes. Then add the fresh cilantro.

- Blend the cornstarch with 2 tablespoons water, pour into the hot curry, and stir well to thicken. Serve with rice and poppadoms.

Pulpy Mango and Chicken Curry

Heat 1 tablespoon oil in a large, heavy skillet over medium heat. Add ¾ lb diced chicken and cook for 2 minutes. Add 2 tablespoons curry paste, 1¼ cups mango pulp and 13½ fl oz can coconut milk. Bring to a boil, reduce the heat, and simmer for 7 minutes. Add 1¾ cups frozen peas for the final 3 minutes of cooking. Serve with toasted naan bread.

Caribbean-Style Chicken, Mango, and Plantain Curry Heat 2 tablespoons oil in a large, heavy skillet or wok over medium heat. Add 1 lb diced chicken meat and 1 large diced onion and cook for 5 minutes. Remove the seed from 1 large mango, chop the flesh, discarding the skin, and add to the pan with ½ lb diced or sliced plantain. Add 1 teaspoon ground coriander, 1 teaspoon ground cumin, and 3 tablespoons curry paste, and cook, stirring, for 1 minute. Add 2 × 13½ fl oz cans coconut milk. Bring to a boil, reduce the heat, cover, and simmer for 20 minutes. Add 5 tablespoons chopped fresh cilantro and stir through. Serve with rice mixed with kidney beans.

Chicken Chili with Potato Wedges and Guacamole

Serves 4

1¾ lb ready-prepared potato wedges

3 tablespoons oil

1 lb ground chicken

1 tablespoon mild chili powder

2 teaspoons ground cumin

2 teaspoons ground coriander

13½ oz can diced tomatoes

¾ cup rich chicken stock

15 oz can red kidney beans, rinsed and drained

1 tablespoon chopped cilantro

For the guacamole

1 ripe avocado

1 tablespoon lemon juice

pinch of chili powder

- Toss the potato wedges in 2 tablespoons of the oil and place in a single layer on a baking pan. Roast in a preheated oven at 425°F for 20–25 minutes, or until lightly golden and cooked through.

- Meanwhile, heat the remaining oil oil in a large, heavy skillet over high heat. Add the ground chicken and cook, stirring frequently, for 10 minutes, or until the chicken is golden in places. Add the chili powder, cumin, and coriander and cook for 2 minutes. Stir in the tomatoes and chicken stock and bring to a boil. Reduce the heat, simmer for 10 minutes, and add the kidney beans. Cook for a further 5 minutes.

- Meanwhile, mash the avocado in a bowl with the lemon juice and stir in the chili powder. Lightly stir the chicken with the potato wedges and place on warmed serving plates. Place spoonfuls of chunky guacamole on the side, scatter everything with cilantro, and serve.

Simple Chunky Chicken Chili with Guacamole Dice 3 cooked chicken breasts, each weighing about ¼ lb, and place in a pan with a 13 oz jar chili sauce, a 9 oz jar roasted red peppers, drained and roughly diced, and a 15 oz can kidney beans, rinsed and drained. Bring to a boil, reduce the heat, and simmer for 7–8 minutes, or until piping hot. Serve with ready-made guacamole and crusty bread.

Chicken Chili with Peppers Heat 2 tablespoons oil in a large, heavy skillet over high heat. Add 1 large diced onion, 1 diced red pepper, and 1 diced orange pepper along with 1 lb ground chicken. Cook for 10 minutes, or until golden. Add 1 tablespoon mild chili powder and a 13 oz jar chili sauce. Bring to a boil, stirring, then reduce the heat and simmer for 5 minutes before serving with chopped fresh cilantro to garnish. Serve with quick-cook rice or naan bread.

QuickCook

Food for Friends

Recipes listed by cooking time

30

20

10

Chicken Breasts with Mushroom Sauce and Walnut Bread Tops 206

Garlic and Herb Stuffed Chicken with Sun-Dried Tomatoes and Prosciutto 208

Sweet Balsamic Chicken with Pan-Fried Onions 210

Yogurt and Harissa Chicken Kebabs 212

Chicken with a Tarragon Cream Sauce and Mushroom Rice 214

Chicken, Shrimp, and Chorizo Pilaf 216

Griddled Chicken Breasts with Blue Cheese Sauce 218

Moroccan-Style Chicken Soup 220

Chicken, Sweet Potato, and Thyme Cannelloni 222

Chicken Breasts with Crème Fraîche and Three-Mustard Sauce 224

Creamy Chicken, Asparagus, and Pine Nut Tagliatelle 226

Cherry Tomato and Garlic Chicken Pan-Fry 180

Greek Salad with Mixed Herb Dressing 182

Chicken Couscous 184

Gazpacho Soup with Chicken Salsa 186

Simple Warm Chicken Liver Pâté 188

Thyme and Sesame Stir-Fry with Chickpeas 190

Chicken, Spinach, and Goat Cheese Tarts 192

Fennel and Chicken Pilaf 194

Panzanella with Chicken 196

Fusilli with Rosemary, Lemon, and Garlic Chicken 198

Smoked Chicken and Salami Wrap 200

Piri-Piri Stir-Fry 202

Chicken, Mushroom, and Red Wine Soup with Croutons 204

Hot Chicken, Mushroom, and Pâté Wraps with Arugula 206

Garlic and Herb Chicken with Sun-Dried Tomatoes and Rice 208

Balsamic Chicken Bruschetta 210

Harissa Chickpea Dip with Chicken 212

Warm Chicken, Tarragon, and Mushroom Salad 214

Chicken, Artichoke, and Green Bean Bruschetta 216

Chicken Breast with Blue Cheese and Mango Chutney 218

Quick Couscous Salad with Moroccan Flavors 220

Chicken, Beet, and Cucumber Salad with Thyme Dressing 222

Creamy Chicken Pan-Fry with Hot Mustard Sauce 224

Broiled Chicken, Asparagus, and Pine Nuts on Spinach Salad 226

Chicken Parmigiana

Serves 4

2 chicken breasts, each weighing about 6 oz, halved lengthwise

2 eggs, beaten

1 cup bread crumbs

¾ cup freshly grated Parmesan cheese

1 tablespoon olive oil

2 garlic cloves, crushed

10½ oz jar tomato sauce or passata

1 teaspoon superfine sugar

1 teaspoon dried oregano

5 oz mozzarella cheese, drained

- Put the chicken breasts between 2 sheets of plastic wrap and beat with a rolling pin until they are ½ inch thick. Dip the chicken in the egg and then in the bread crumbs mixed with half the Parmesan. Set aside on a plate in the refrigerator.

- Meanwhile, heat the oil in a large, heavy skillet over medium heat. Add the garlic and fry for a few seconds, then add the tomato sauce or passata, sugar, and oregano. Simmer for 5–8 minutes until thick and pulpy.

- Cook the chicken under a preheated hot broiler for 5 minutes on each side until pale golden. Pour the tomato sauce into a shallow, ovenproof gratin dish and set the chicken on top. Scatter with the mozzarella and remaining Parmesan and broil for 3–4 minutes until the cheese has melted and the sauce is bubbling. Serve with salad or vegetables, if liked.

---

1 Cherry Tomato and Garlic Chicken

Pan-Fry Heat 2 tablespoons olive oil in a large, heavy skillet over high heat. Add ½ lb diced chicken and cook for 3 minutes. Add 1 cup whole cherry tomatoes and stir-fry for a further 5 minutes. Add 1 teaspoon minced garlic, ¾ cup pitted |black olives and ¾ cup tomato sauce or passata, and cook for a further minute until piping hot. Serve in warmed bowls with plenty of freshly grated Parmesan cheese and warm crusty bread.

2 Chicken and Tomato Pasta

Gratin Cook ½ lb pasta shapes in a large saucepan of lightly salted boiling water for 8–10 minutes, or until al dente. Meanwhile, heat 3 tablespoons olive oil in a large, heavy saucepan over high heat. Add 2 thinly sliced chicken breasts, each weighing about 5 oz, and cook for 5 minutes, or until golden. Add 1 crushed garlic clove and a 1 lb 8 oz jar tomato sauce or passata and 1 teaspoon dried oregano and bring to a boil. Drain the pasta and stir into the chicken and tomato sauce. Transfer to a large, shallow ovenproof dish and scatter with 1 cup fresh bread crumbs mixed with ¾ cup freshly grated Parmesan cheese. Place under a preheated hot broiler and cook for 3–4 minutes, or until golden and bubbling.

Greek-Style Chicken Thighs with Olives and Green Beans

Serves 4

2 tablespoons olive oil

4 chicken thighs

1 large red onion, sliced

1½ cups cherry tomatoes, halved

13½ oz can diced tomatoes with garlic and herbs

4 tablespoons sun-dried tomato paste

¾ cup kalamata olives, drained

¾ cup red wine

6 oz green beans, trimmed

2 oz feta cheese, crumbled, to serve

- Heat the oil in large, heavy skillet over high heat. Add the chicken thighs and red onion and cook for 5 minutes, turning once, until golden.

- Add the cherry tomatoes and stir-fry for 2 minutes, then add the diced tomatoes and tomato paste and bring to a boil. Reduce the heat, cover, and simmer for 15 minutes. Add the wine and the beans and stir. Cover the pan again and cook for 5 minutes more, or until the beans are just tender and the chicken is cooked through.

- Ladle into warmed bowls and scatter with the crumbled feta to serve. Accompany with warm continental crusty bread to mop up the juices, if liked.

10 **Greek Salad with Mixed Herb Dressing** Chop ½ cucumber into chunks and put in a salad bowl with ½ lb sliced cooked chicken, 1½ cups baby cherry tomatoes, halved, and ¾ cup kalamata olives. Toss together well. Make a dressing by whisking together 4 tablespoons olive oil, 2 tablespoons red wine vinegar, 1 teaspoon Dijon mustard, and ½ teaspoon dried mixed herbs. Pour the dressing over the salad ingredients and toss well to coat.

20 **Greek-Style Mixed Olive, Chicken, and Tomato Pizza** Put a ready-made 9 inch pizza crust onto a pizza pan and spread 3 tablespoons sun-dried tomato paste over the top. Scatter with ¼ lb sliced cooked chicken, 1 cup cherry tomatoes, halved, and ¾ cup mixed assorted olives, including kalamata black olives. Scatter evenly with 1¼ cup grated mozzarella cheese and then 2 oz feta cheese, finely crumbled. Bake in the top of a preheated oven at 425°F for 10–12 minutes, or until golden and bubbling. Serve drizzled with olive oil.

Gingered Chicken, Seed, and Vegetable Rice

Serves 4

1¼ cups quick-cooking brown rice

2 tablespoons olive oil

10 oz diced chicken

1 tablespoon ginger paste

1 onion, thinly sliced

4 tablespoons sunflower seeds

3 tablespoons pumpkin seeds

1 tablespoon black mustard seeds

1 large zucchini, grated

1 large carrot, grated

1¼ cups petit pois

- Cook the rice in a large saucepan of lightly salted boiling water for 15 minutes, or until tender.

- Meanwhile, put 1 tablespoon of the oil in a large mixing bowl with the chicken and ginger paste and mix well to lightly coat the chicken. Add the chicken and onion to a large, heavy skillet over medium heat and cook, stirring occasionally, for 10 minutes, or until golden in places and cooked through.

- Meanwhile, in another skillet heat the remaining oil and cook the seeds for 1 minute to brown a little. Add the zucchini and carrot. Stir-fry for 3 minutes until softened, add the petit pois, and stir-fry for a further 2–3 minutes until piping hot.

- Drain the rice and add to the skillet with the chicken. Toss well then add the hot seeds, zucchini, carrots, and petit pois and toss again. Serve hot in warmed serving bowls.

Chicken Couscous Make 3½ oz lemon-and-cilantro-flavored couscous according to the instructions on the package and set aside to swell. Meanwhile, set a large, heavy skillet over high heat. Toss ¾ lb diced chicken with 1 tablespoon ginger paste and 1 tablespoon olive oil. Add to the hot pan and cook, stirring occasionally, for 8 minutes, or until golden and cooked through. Toss the chicken with the couscous and 4 tablespoons chopped fresh cilantro and serve immediately.

Gingered Chicken Pilaf with Roasted Vegetables Roughly chop 2 large zucchini and 2 large carrots, and cut 2 red onions into thin wedges. Place them in a roasting pan with 4 tablespoons olive oil and toss in the oil to coat. Roast in a preheated oven at 400°F for 20 minutes until tender and lightly charred in places. Meanwhile, bring a large pan of lightly salted water to a boil and cook 1¼ cups rice for 15 minutes or until tender, then drain. Now toss ¾ lb diced chicken with 1 tablespoon olive oil and 1 tablespoon ginger paste then cook in a large, heavy preheated skillet for 10 minutes, or until cooked through and golden. Toss the rice, roasted vegetables, and chicken together in the skillet. Scatter with 4 tablespoons chopped fresh cilantro before serving.

Broiled Gazpacho Chicken Salad

Serves 4

6 tablespoons olive oil

4 tablespoons finely chopped basil

3 chicken breasts, each weighing about 5 oz

5½ oz drained piquante peppers from a jar

1 bunch of scallions, roughly diced

½ cucumber, roughly diced

1½ cups baby plum tomatoes, halved

4 tablespoons chopped flat-leaf parsley

- Whisk 2 tablespoons of the oil in a shallow bowl with 3 tablespoons of the basil. Brush the mixture over the chicken breasts. Arrange the chicken on the rack of a foil-lined broiler pan. Place under a preheated hot broiler and cook for 5–6 minutes on each side, or until golden and cooked through.

- Meanwhile, put the piquante peppers in a large salad bowl with the scallions, cucumber, baby plum tomatoes, and parsley and toss together. Add the remaining oil and the remaining basil and toss again.

- Cut the hot chicken into thin slices, add to the salad, and toss to mix. Serve with warm crusty bread, if liked.

Gazpacho Soup with Chicken Salsa

Put 4 quartered tomatoes in a food processor or blender with 3 drained piquante peppers, 4 diced scallions, and ¼ roughly diced cucumber. Process until thick and smooth. Add a 13½ oz can diced tomatoes and blend again. Meanwhile, chop 1 cooked chicken breast, about ¼ lb in weight, into small pieces and mix with 1 tablespoon chopped parsley. Ladle the cold soup into 4 serving bowls and place a spoonful of chicken salsa on top of each.

Gazpacho Chicken Bake with Cucumber and Piquante Salsa

Toss 4 chicken breasts, each weighing about ¼ lb, in 2 tablespoons olive oil, 2 tablespoons chopped basil, and plenty of pepper. Transfer to a large roasting pan, add 2½ cups cherry tomatoes, halved, and drizzle with 2 tablespoons olive oil. Season with ½ teaspoon salt flakes and pepper. Toss 1½ cups fresh white bread crumbs with 4 tablespoons chopped parsley and 4 tablespoons freshly grated Parmesan cheese and scatter evenly onto the chicken and tomatoes. Roast in a preheated oven at 425°F for 20 minutes, or until the chicken is golden and the cherry tomatoes are soft. Meanwhile, make a salsa by combining ¼ finely diced cucumber, 1 small minced red chile, 4 finely diced piquante peppers, and 3 tablespoons chopped parsley. Serve the hot gazpacho chicken bake with spoonfuls of salsa on top.

CHI-FOOD-WYQ

Simple Warm Chicken Liver Pâté

Serves 4

2 tablespoons butter
¾ lb chicken livers,
   well drained
1 onion, roughly diced
1 tablespoon sherry
1 tablespoon chopped thyme
   leaves (optional)
pepper

- Heat the butter in a large, heavy skillet over high heat. Add the chicken livers and onion and cook for 7–8 minutes, or until softened and golden. Add the sherry and shake the pan to mix.

- Put the chicken and onion in a food processor or blender and process until creamy and smooth. Season generously with pepper and stir through 1 tablespoon chopped thyme leaves, if liked.

- Serve spooned onto serving plates with warm toast, salad, and ready-made onion chutney.

20 Chicken Liver Salad with Walnuts

Heat 2 tablespoons olive oil in a large, heavy skillet over high heat. Add 1 sliced red onion and ¾ lb well-drained chicken livers. Cook for 8–10 minutes, or until golden and soft. Add 1 cup walnut pieces and cook for a further 2 minutes. Put 4–5 cups salad leaves in a salad bowl with ¾ cup baby plum tomatoes, halved, and add the warm chicken livers, onion, and walnuts. Whisk together 3 tablespoons olive oil and 2 tablespoons balsamic vinegar and pour it over the salad. Toss and serve immediately.

30 Warm Chicken Liver Terrine

with Pistachios Cook 1 lb well-drained chicken livers, 6 slices of smoked Canadian bacon, diced, and 1 diced onion in a large, heavy skillet over high heat for 8–10 minutes, or until golden and soft. Add 2 tablespoons brandy, stir, and remove from the heat. Transfer the mixture to a food processor or blender and process until smooth. Add to a mixing bowl with 1 cup roughly chopped pistachios and mix. Line a 1 lb loaf pan with plastic wrap, spoon the warm mixture into the pan, and press down well. Turn the warm terrine onto a serving plate and garnish with thyme leaves. Serve in slices with toasted dinner rolls.

CHI-FOOD-HOS

Sesame and Thyme Skewers with Spicy Mashed Chickpeas

Serves 4

3 chicken breasts, each weighing about 5 oz, cut into small chunks

3 tablespoons sesame oil

1 tablespoon chopped thyme leaves

2 tablespoons sesame seeds

2 tablespoons olive oil

1 onion, diced

1 small red chile, minced

2 thyme sprigs, plus extra to garnish (optional)

2 × 15½ oz cans chickpeas, rinsed and drained

6 tablespoons hot chicken stock

salt and pepper

- Put the chicken chunks in a bowl with the sesame oil, thyme leaves, and sesame seeds and toss to coat. Thread the chicken evenly onto 8 skewers and arrange on the rack of a foil-lined broiler pan. Place under a preheated broiler and cook, turning frequently, for 10 minutes, or until golden and cooked through.

- Meanwhile, heat the oil in a heavy skillet over medium-high heat. Add the onion, chile, and thyme sprigs and cook for 3–4 minutes, or until the onion is soft and becoming golden. Add the chickpeas. Heat, stirring, for 1 minute, then add the stock. Cover the pan with a lid, bring to a boil, and cook for 3 minutes until piping hot. Season well. Transfer to a food processor or blender and process until almost smooth but still holding some texture.

- Serve the mashed chickpeas in bowls with chicken skewers on the side garnished with thyme sprigs, if liked.

 Thyme and Sesame Stir-Fry with Chickpeas Heat 1 tablespoon sesame oil in a large, heavy skillet over high heat. Add ¾ lb diced chicken and cook for 3–4 minutes. Add ½ teaspoon dried thyme leaves and 2 tablespoons sesame seeds and continue to stir-fry for 2 minutes. Add 1 sliced red chile and 2 × 15½ oz cans chickpeas. Cook, stirring, for a further 2 minutes until piping hot. Scatter with 4 tablespoons chopped fresh cilantro leaves before serving.

Minted Yogurt Chicken Skewers with Warm Chickpea Salad Cut 4 chicken breasts into pieces and put them in a bowl with a mixture of 2 teaspoons ground coriander, 1 teaspoon ground cumin, 1½ cups plain yogurt, the juice of ½ lemon, 1 tablespoon olive oil, 1 crushed garlic clove, and 2 tablespoons chopped mint leaves. Mix well to coat. Thread the chicken evenly onto 8 bamboo or metal skewers. Place them on the rack of a foil-lined broiler pan and cook under a preheated moderate broiler, turning regularly, for 15 minutes. Meanwhile, thinly slice 1 onion. Heat 2 tablespoons olive oil and cook the onion over a medium-high heat with 1 teaspoon cumin seeds for 3–4 minutes, or until beginning to soften. Add 1 small minced red chile and continue to cook for a further 1 minute before adding 2 × 15½ oz cans drained chickpeas. Add 6 tablespoons chicken stock or water, cover, and simmer for 2–3 minutes, or until piping hot. Scatter with 5 tablespoons chopped fresh cilantro and spoon onto warm serving plates with the minted chicken skewers on top to serve.

Chicken, Spinach, Onion Chutney, and Goat Cheese Tarts

Serves 4

12 oz sheet puff pastry, cut into 4 equal rectangles

2 tablespoons olive oil

½ lb chicken, diced

7 oz fresh spinach

½ teaspoon ground nutmeg

1 teaspoon mustard seeds

8 tablespoons ready-made red or white onion chutney

8 thick slices goat cheese, rind removed

salt and pepper

- Put the 4 pastry sheets on a large baking pan and prick all over with a fork.

- Heat the oil in a large, heavy skillet over high heat. Add the chicken and cook for 3 minutes. Stir in the spinach leaves and cook for 1 minute until wilted. Remove from the heat, add the nutmeg and mustard seeds, and season with a little salt and pepper, tossing well to coat.

- Drain the mixture if necessary, then spoon evenly onto the 4 sheets of pastry to within 1 inch of the edges. Spoon 2 tablespoons of onion chutney over the top of each and put 2 slices goat cheese on top of the chutney. Bake in a preheated oven at 425°F for 20 minutes, or until puffed and golden. Serve with a simple salad.

1. Chicken, Spinach, and Goat Cheese Tarts

Heat 1 tablespoon olive oil and 1 tablespoon butter in a large, heavy skillet. Add ½ lb diced chicken and cook for 5 minutes. Stir in 3 cups fresh spinach cook for 2 minutes. Add ½ teaspoon ground nutmeg and season well. Discard the rind from 2 oz goat cheese and cut the cheese into small cubes. Stir these into the chicken and spinach. Spoon the mixture into 4 ready-made single-serving pie crusts and serve with salad.

2. Chicken, Spinach, and Goat Cheese Pizza

Put a ready-made 9 inch pizza crust on a pizza pan and cook under a preheated medium broiler for 2 minutes until warm. Meanwhile, heat 2 tablespoons olive oil in a large, heavy skillet over high heat. Add 6 oz diced chicken and cook for 3 minutes. Stir in 7 oz fresh spinach and ½ teaspoon nutmeg and cook for 1 minute, or until the spinach has wilted. Arrange on top of the pizza crust then spread 8 teaspoons onion chutney evenly on top of the spinach. Then arrange 6 slices of goat cheese, rind removed, evenly over the pizza. Place under the broiler, not too close to the element, and cook for 5–6 minutes, or until the topping is warm and the cheese is melted and golden.

 Chicken and Fennel Risotto with Vermouth

Serves 4

3 tablespoons olive oil

3½ tablespoons butter

1 onion, thinly sliced

1 fennel head, trimmed and thinly sliced

1 chicken breast, weighing about 5 oz, finely sliced into strips

1 teaspoon fennel seeds, roughly crushed

1 cup easy-cook risotto rice

3 tablespoons vermouth

2½ cups rich chicken stock

freshly grated Parmesan cheese, to serve

arugula, to garnish

- Heat the oil and butter in a large, heavy skillet over medium-high heat. Add the onion and fennel and cook, stirring occasionally, for 5 minutes, or until softened and golden in places. Add the chicken and fennel seeds and stir-fry for a further 2 minutes.

- Add the rice and vermouth to the pan. Increase the heat for a few seconds to burn off the alcohol, stirring continuously, then add half the chicken stock. Cook, stirring occasionally, on medium heat until almost all the stock has been absorbed, then add the remaining stock and continue to cook in the same way for about 10–15 minutes, reducing the heat to a simmer, until the rice is tender and cooked but still with a slight bite.

- Serve in warmed bowls with plenty of freshly grated Parmesan, a small handful of arugula on top to garnish, and warm crusty bread on the side, if liked.

 Fennel and Chicken Pilaf

Heat 2 tablespoons olive oil in a large, heavy skillet over high heat. Add 1 roughly diced, trimmed fennel head along with ½ lb diced chicken meat and cook for 5 minutes, or until softened and golden. Add 1 roughly diced bunch of scallions and ½ teaspoon fennel seeds and continue to cook for a further minute. Add 1¼ cup quick-cooking rice and continue stir-frying for a further 2 minutes until piping hot. Serve with an arugula salad.

 Chicken, Bacon, and Fennel Risotto with Roasted Butternut Squash

Peel and roughly chop a 1 lb butternut squash, toss in 2 tablespoons olive oil, and roast in a preheated oven at 400°F for 20 minutes until softened and lightly charred. Meanwhile, make the risotto as above, adding 4 slices of bacon, diced, to the pan with the chicken and cooking for the same length of time. Once the risotto is cooked, fold in the butternut squash and serve with arugula.

Panzanella with Chicken

Serves 4

½ ciabatta loaf, torn into pieces
4 tablespoons olive oil
½ cucumber, roughly diced
2 large tomatoes, roughly diced
2 cooked chicken breasts, about
  ½ lb in total, torn into pieces
1 small red onion, roughly diced
8 tablespoons ready-made
  French dressing
2 tablespoons chopped basil
salt and pepper

- Put the ciabatta pieces in a roasting pan and drizzle with the olive oil. Place under a preheated hot broiler for 2–3 minutes and cook until golden and warm.

- Meanwhile, put the cucumber, tomatoes, chicken, onion, and dressing in a large mixing bowl. Add the chopped basil and mix well. Season with salt and black pepper.

- Add the warm ciabatta pieces to the bowl and toss well to coat in the dressing. Serve with extra French dressing, if liked.

Chicken, Tomato, and Zucchini

Bruschetta Heat 2 tablespoons olive oil in a large skillet over high heat. Add 2 thinly sliced chicken breasts, each weighing about 5 oz, and cook for 5 minutes. Add 1 diced zucchini and cook for a further 5 minutes before adding 2 roughly diced tomatoes and 1 tablespoon chopped rosemary leaves. Cook for 2–3 minutes, or until the tomatoes are soft yet still retain their shape. Meanwhile, cut ¼ ciabatta loaf into as wide slices as possible on an angle and lightly brush each side with a little olive oil. Heat a ridged griddle pan and cook the bread slices for 30 seconds on each side. Place on warmed serving plates and spoon the warm chicken on top to serve.

Zucchini and Tomato Bake

Heat 4 tablespoons olive oil in a large skillet over high heat. Add ¾ lb diced chicken and cook for 5 minutes. Add 1 large roughly diced zucchini and 1 roughly diced red onion and cook for a further 5 minutes. Add a 1 lb jar or can of ready-made tomato pasta sauce with herbs and heat for 1–2 minutes until hot. Transfer to a large, shallow ovenproof gratin dish and scatter with the ¼ roughly torn ciabatta loaf. Drizzle with 1 tablespoon olive oil. Bake in a preheated oven at 400°F for 15 minutes, or until the top is pale golden and the sauce is bubbling. Serve with a simple salad or green vegetables.

Lemon and Garlic Chicken Breasts with Rosemary Gravy

Serves 4

4 chicken breasts, each weighing about 5 oz (with skin on)

1 lemon, sliced

4 rosemary sprigs

8 garlic cloves, peeled

2 tablespoons olive oil

salt and pepper

For the gravy

1 tablespoon olive oil

1 tablespoon chopped rosemary leaves

1¼ cups chicken stock

6 tablespoons white wine

2 teaspoons cornstarch

green beans and boiled potatoes, to serve

- Make a large slit in the side of each chicken breast and insert 2 slices of lemon, 1 rosemary sprig, and a halved garlic clove. Tie each chicken with kitchen string around the center, then arrange in a roasting pan. Drizzle with olive oil and season generously with salt and pepper. Roast in a preheated oven at 425°F for 20–25 minutes, or until golden and cooked through.

- Meanwhile, make the gravy. Heat the oil in a small saucepan over medium heat. Add the rosemary leaves and cook for 1 minute. Pour in the stock and wine and bring to a boil. Continue to boil for 5 minutes to infuse the flavors and reduce a little. Blend the cornstarch with 2 tablespoons water and add to the gravy, stirring continually to thicken. Pour over the roasted chicken pieces and serve with green beans and boiled potatoes.

Fusilli with Rosemary, Lemon, and Garlic Chicken Cook 8 oz fusilli in a large saucepan of lightly salted boiling water for 8–10 minutes, or until tender. Meanwhile, heat 6 tablespoons garlic-infused olive oil in a large, heavy skillet over high heat. Add ½ lb diced chicken and cook for 5 minutes. Add 2 tablespoons chopped rosemary and cook for 2 minutes. Drain the pasta well and add to the pan with the chicken and rosemary. Add the grated zest and juice of 1 lemon. Toss well and serve hot.

 Chicken, Lemon, and Rosemary Risotto Heat 2 tablespoons olive oil in a large, heavy skillet over high heat. Add ½ lb diced chicken with 1 minced garlic clove and 1 tablespoon chopped rosemary and cook for 5 minutes. Add 1 cup quick-cooking long-grain rice with the finely grated zest and juice of 1 lemon and 2½ cups chicken stock. Bring to a boil, cover, and simmer, stirring, for 12–15 minutes, or until the rice is tender and cooked. Serve spooned into warmed serving bowls with an arugula salad.

CHI-FOOD-MEW

Smoked Chicken, Tomato, and Salami Calzone

Serves 4

7 oz pizza crust mix

¼ lb smoked chicken, chopped

½ cup cherry tomatoes, quartered

3 oz Milano salami, roughly chopped

1 tablespoon chopped parsley

4 tablespoons passata or tomato sauce

dressed green salad, to serve (optional)

- Make the pizza crust according to the instructions on the package. Turn the dough out onto a lightly floured surface and knead for 1–2 minutes until smooth. Divide the dough into 4 pieces and knead each a little to form smooth, round balls. Roll each out to a disk about 6 inches across.

- Mix together the chicken, cherry tomatoes, salami, parsley, and passata and divide the mixture evenly among the disks, spooning it into the center. Lightly brush the edges of each disk with a little water and then fold one side over to meet the other. Press together to form 4 half-moon shapes. Place on a baking pan and bake at the top of a preheated oven at 425°F for 15 minutes, or until pale golden. Serve with a simple green salad dressed with olive oil and balsamic vinegar, if liked.

1   Smoked Chicken and Salami Wrap

Put 4 tortilla wraps on a cutting board and spread each one with 1 tablespoon sun-dried tomato paste. Arrange 2 oz thinly sliced Milano salami on top of each and then scatter with 1 oz smoked chicken. Put 3 cups arugula in a bowl with 1 tablespoon olive oil, 1 tablespoon balsamic vinegar, and 6 quartered cherry tomatoes and toss well. Arrange the salad evenly on top of the chicken, roll up tightly, and cut each wrap in two, securing with a toothpick. Serve cold.

2   Savory Smoked Crêpes

Make 3½ oz batter mix according to the instructions on the package. Heat a skillet until hot and grease with a little oil. Pour ¼ of the pancake batter into the pan and cook for about 1 minute, flip, and cook on the other side for a few seconds until golden. Repeat using the remaining batter to make 4 pancakes. Put ¾ cup passata in a pan with 4 oz chopped Milano salami, 4 oz chopped smoked chicken, and 8 halved cherry tomatoes. Heat for 2–3 minutes until piping hot then use the mixture to fill the crêpes, folding them in triangles or rolling them up. Place in a shallow, ovenproof dish in a single layer and scatter evenly with ½ cup grated Parmesan cheese. Place under a preheated hot broiler and cook for 1–2 minutes or until golden. Serve with a simply dressed green salad.

CHI-FOOD-HUJ

Piri-Piri Stir-Fry

Serves 4

2 tablespoons olive oil
1 lb chicken tenders
thyme sprigs, to garnish

For the piri-piri sauce

1 teaspoon minced red chile
1 teaspoon minced garlic
¼ teaspoon dried oregano
¼ teaspoon dried thyme
1 teaspoon paprika
2 tablespoons red wine vinegar

To serve

quick-cooking rice
green salad

- Heat the oil in a large, heavy wok or skillet over high heat. Add the chicken and cook, stirring occasionally, for 5 minutes, or until golden in places.

- Meanwhile, mix together all the ingredients for the piri-piri sauce and add to the pan with the chicken. Stir-fry for a further 3–4 minutes, stirring occasionally, until the sauce flavors the chicken and the chicken is cooked through. Garnish with fresh thyme sprigs.

- Serve hot with quick-cooking rice and a crisp green salad.

20 Piri-Piri Chicken and Pepper Kebabs

Cut 3 chicken breasts, each weighing about 5 oz, into cubes and cut 1 large red pepper into chunks. Thread onto 8 bamboo or metal skewers and place on a the rack of a foil-lined broiler pan. Mix together 2 tablespoons olive oil, 1 teaspoon minced garlic, 1 teaspoon minced chile, ½ teaspoon dried oregano, and ¼ teaspoon dried thyme to make a paste. Add 1 teaspoon paprika and 1 tablespoon red wine vinegar and mix again. Brush the paste over the kebabs. Heat a ridged griddle pan and cook the kebabs over high heat for 2–3 minutes on each side until golden and lightly charred in places.

30 Piri-Piri Chicken Thighs with

Griddled Peppers Make 2 deep slashes in 8 chicken thighs. Place them on a preheated ridged griddle pan and cook for 5 minutes on each side. Meanwhile, mix together 1 minced red chile, 3 tablespoons olive oil, 1 minced or crushed garlic clove, ½ teaspoon dried oregano, the grated zest and juice of 1 lemon, 1 teaspoon paprika, and 2 tablespoons red wine vinegar. Put the chicken thighs in a roasting pan and liberally brush with the marinade, then roast at the top of a preheated oven at 400°F for 15 minutes. Meanwhile, cut a red pepper into strips and cook,

turning occasionally, on the griddle pan for 5 minutes, or until softened and cooked. Serve the chicken with the peppers, garnished with thyme sprigs.

CHI-FOOD-QIS

30 Quick Coq au Vin

Serves 4

2 tablespoons olive oil
8 chicken drumsticks
8 slices bacon, roughly diced
8 whole shallots
½ lb crimini mushrooms, halved
1 tablespoon all-purpose flour
2 tablespoons thyme leaves
1¼ cups red wine
2 cups rich chicken stock
thyme sprigs, to garnish
mashed potatoes, to serve

- Heat the oil in a large, heavy skillet over high heat. Add the drumsticks and bacon and cook for 5 minutes. Then add the shallots and mushrooms and cook for a further 5 minutes, turning the chicken and shallots, until golden all over. Add the flour and toss to coat, then add the thyme.

- Pour in the wine and stock and bring to a boil, stirring continually to distribute the flour evenly within the sauce. Reduce the heat and simmer, uncovered, for 15 minutes, or until the chicken is cooked through.

- Garnish the coq au vin with thyme sprigs and serve ladled onto hot mashed potatoes in warmed serving bowls.

---

10 Chicken, Mushroom, and Red Wine Soup with Croutons

Heat 1 tablespoon olive oil in a pan over high heat. Add 6 oz diced chicken with 1 diced onion and 1½ cups roughly diced mushrooms and cook for 5 minutes. Meanwhile, make ¼ cup red wine sauce according to the instructions on the package and add to the chicken, along with 1¼ cups chicken stock. Bring to a boil, ladle into warmed serving bowls, and serve scattered with ready-made croutons.

20 Coq au Vin Style Chicken Breasts

Heat 1 tablespoon olive oil in a large, heavy skillet over medium heat. Add 4 chicken breasts, each weighing about ¼ lb, and 1 small sliced red onion. Cook for 10 minutes, turning the chicken once. Meanwhile, in a separate pan heat 1 tablespoon olive oil and add 4 slices of bacon, diced, with 2 cups halved chestnut mushrooms. Cook for 5 minutes. Add the mushrooms and bacon to the pan with the chicken. Stir in ¾ cup red wine and 1¼ cups rich chicken stock and bring to a boil. Reduce the heat, cover, and simmer for 5 minutes. Blend 1 teaspoon cornstarch with 1 tablespoon water, add to the sauce, and stir well to thicken. Serve on a bed of instant mashed potatoes.

Chicken, Porcini Mushroom, and Pâté Pies

Serves 4

1½ oz dried porcini mushrooms, diced

8 oz sheet puff pastry

beaten egg, to glaze

4 chicken breasts, each weighing about ¼ lb

4 oz Ardennes pâté

2 tablespoons butter

¾ cup white wine

¾ cup heavy cream

2 tablespoons chopped parsley, to garnish

- Soak the porcini mushrooms in ¾ cup boiling water for 10 minutes.

- Cut the puff pastry into 4 diamond shapes and make 3 small incisions in the top. Place on a baking pan, brush with beaten egg, and cook in a preheated oven at 400°F for 12–15 minutes, or until golden and puffed.

- Meanwhile, make large slits in the side of each chicken breast. Cut the pâté into 4 slices and put a slice inside each chicken breast. Divide the mushrooms in half. Put one-quarter of one-half inside each chicken breast and tie with kitchen string. Heat the butter in a large skillet over high heat. Add the breasts and cook for 5 minutes on each side until golden.

- Pour in the white wine and remaining mushrooms and bring to a boil. Reduce the heat, turn the chicken breasts over, cover, and simmer for 5 minutes. Transfer the chicken to 4 warmed serving plates. Add the cream to the pan, heat for 1 minute, and spoon over the chicken. Place a pastry diamond on each plate and garnish with chopped parsley to serve.

Hot Chicken, Mushroom, and Pâté Wraps with Arugula

Heat 3 tablespoons olive oil in a large skillet over medium heat. Add 2 thinly sliced chicken breasts, together with 2 cups quartered crimini mushrooms. Cook for 7–8 minutes, or until golden. Spread 2 tablespoons pâté each on 4 flour tortillas and place a handful of arugula on top. Scatter with the hot chicken and mushrooms, roll up tightly, and cut each in half to serve.

Chicken Breasts with Mushroom Sauce and Walnut Bread Tops

Soak 1 oz porcini mushrooms in ¾ cup boiling water and set aside for 10 minutes. Put 2 tablespoons olive oil in a skillet over high heat and add 4 chicken breasts, each weighing about ¼ lb, and cook for 5 minutes on each side. Add 2 cups quartered crimini mushrooms, the porcini mushrooms, drained and diced, and ¾ cup white wine. Bring to a boil, reduce the heat, cover, and simmer for 5 minutes. Meanwhile, toast 4 slices of walnut bread until crisp and golden. Transfer the chicken breasts to 4 warmed serving plates. Add ½ cup heavy cream to the pan and bring to a boil. Spoon the sauce over the chicken and place a slice of toasted walnut bread on top of each portion to serve.

Garlic and Herb Stuffed Chicken with Sun-Dried Tomatoes and Prosciutto

Serves 4

4 chicken breasts, each weighing about ¼ lb

8 sun-dried tomatoes in oil, drained

½ cup garlic and herb soft cheese

8 slices of prosciutto

3 tablespoons olive oil

8 tablespoons white wine

pepper

- Make a deep cut in the side of each chicken breast, almost cutting them in half widthwise, and fill each one with one-quarter of the garlic and herb soft cheese and 2 sun-dried tomatoes. Press down firmly and wrap tightly with 2 slices of prosciutto to hold the sides together.

- Add the oil to a large, heavy skillet over high heat. Add the chicken and cook, seam-side down, for 3–4 minutes on each side, or until golden. Add the wine to the pan, cover with a tight-fitting lid, and cook for a further 5 minutes, or until tender. Season the chicken generously with pepper and arrange on warmed plates. Drizzle the chicken with any pan juices to serve.

Garlic and Herb Chicken with Sun-Dried Tomatoes and Rice

Heat 2 tablespoons olive oil in a large, heavy skillet over high heat. Add ¾ lb diced chicken and cook for 7–8 minutes, or until golden and cooked through. Drain ¾ cup sun-dried tomatoes in oil, add them to the pan, and toss with the chicken. Mix ¾ cup garlic and herb soft cheese with 8 tablespoons milk and stir into the pan. Heat through gently, stirring continually with a wooden spoon, for 1–2 minutes until hot but not boiling. Serve with quick-cooking rice.

Garlic and Herb Chicken en Papilotte

Make a deep cut in the side of each of 4 chicken breasts, each weighing about ¼ lb, and fill each one with about 2 tablespoons garlic and herb soft cheese and 2 sun-dried tomatoes in oil, drained. Wrap each stuffed breast in 2 slices of prosciutto and place each one on a piece of aluminum foil. Fold the foil up around the chicken to form a container and pour 3 tablespoons white wine into each one. Slice 1 onion and scatter over the chicken. Wrap the foil up and over to form a parcel. Transfer to a roasting pan and cook in a preheated oven at 400°F for 20 minutes, unwrapping the foil for the final 5 minutes of cooking to allow the prosciutto to brown a little. Serve with green beans and mashed potatoes.

Sweet Balsamic Chicken with Pan-Fried Onions

Serves 4

6 tablespoons balsamic vinegar

4 chicken breasts, each weighing about 5 oz

2 tablespoons olive oil

1 onion, thinly sliced

1 red onion, thinly sliced

2 tablespoons clear honey

1 tablespoon chopped rosemary

¾ cup chicken stock

pepper

To serve

mashed potatoes

green beans

- Put the balsamic vinegar in a bowl and season with pepper. Make 3 small cuts in the top of each of the chicken breasts. Add the chicken to the vinegar and toss to coat. Set aside for 3–4 minutes.

- Meanwhile, add the oil to a large, heavy skillet over medium-high heat and cook the onions for 5 minutes, or until soft and beginning to turn golden. Add the chicken, cut-side down (reserve the vinegar), and cook for 3 minutes. Turn the chicken over and cook for 3 minutes more.

- Turn once more and add the balsamic vinegar from the bowl together with the honey and rosemary. Reduce the heat, add the stock, cover, and simmer, stirring once, for 3–4 minutes further, or until the chicken is cooked through. Set the chicken on warmed plates and place the onion slices on top. Serve with mashed potatoes and green beans.

10 Balsamic Chicken Bruschetta

Thinly slice 2 chicken breasts, each weighing about ¼ lb, and put in a bowl with 3 tablespoons balsamic vinegar, 1 tablespoon clear honey, and ½ teaspoon dried rosemary. Toss together. Put 1 tablespoon olive oil in a large skillet over high heat. Add the chicken and cook for 7–8 minutes until golden and cooked through. Meanwhile, slice 8 large mushrooms and add to the pan for the final 4 minutes of cooking. Lightly toast 4 slices of ciabatta bread, spoon some balsamic chicken and mushroom onto each slice, and serve warm.

30 Sweet Balsamic Chicken with Roasted Butternut and Peppers

Toss 3 cups butternut squash chunks and 1 red pepper, also cut into chunks, with 2 tablespoons olive oil and 2 tablespoons chopped parsley. Toss 2 chicken breasts, each weighing about ¼ lb, with 4 tablespoons balsamic vinegar and 1 tablespoon clear honey. Put the chicken and vegetables in a roasting pan and cook at the top of a preheated oven at 425°F for 20 minutes, or until golden in places and cooked through. Scatter the chicken and vegetables with 1 tablespoon chopped rosemary leaves and serve with creamy mashed potato, if liked.

 # Harissa Chicken

Serves 4

3 tablespoons olive oil

1 large onion, roughly diced

3 chicken breasts, each weighing about 5 oz, sliced

½ teaspoon ground cinnamon

1 teaspoon ground cumin

1 teaspoon ground coriander

2 tablespoons harissa

13½ oz can diced tomatoes

¾ cup hot chicken stock

15½ oz can chickpeas, rinsed and drained

couscous, to serve (optional)

- Place the oil in a large, heavy wok or skillet over high heat. Add the onion and chicken and cook for 5 minutes. Scatter with the spices and cook, stirring, for 2 minutes.

- Stir in the harissa and continue to cook for 2 further minutes before adding the diced tomatoes and stock. Bring to a boil, reduce the heat, cover, and simmer gently for 15 minutes, stirring occasionally.

- Add the drained chickpeas and cook for a further 2 minutes until piping hot. Serve with couscous fluffed with a fork and drizzled with olive oil, if liked.

1 Harissa Chickpea Dip with Chicken

Put 1 tablespoon olive oil in a skillet over high heat. Add 1 diced onion and 1 small, roughly chopped chicken breast. Cook for 5 minutes, or until golden and soft. Add 1 tablespoon harissa, ½ teaspoon ground cumin, and ½ teaspoon ground coriander. Add 15½ oz can rinsed and drained chickpeas and ¼ cup water. Heat for a further 2 minutes, then transfer to a food processor or blender and process until smooth. Place in a serving large bowl and offer breadsticks and sugar snap peas for dipping.

2 Yogurt and Harissa Chicken Kebabs

Cube 3 chicken breasts, each weighing about 5 oz. Put them in a bowl with 4 tablespoons plain yogurt, 1 tablespoon harissa, a pinch each of cinnamon, cumin, and coriander, and 2 tablespoons chopped fresh cilantro. Toss well to coat the chicken. Thread onto 4 bamboo skewers and place on the rack of a foil-lined broiler pan along with ¾ cup cherry tomatoes. Place under a preheated broiler and cook, turning once, for 8–10 minutes, or until lightly charred and cooked through. Serve with couscous fluffed up with a fork.

Chicken with a Tarragon Cream Sauce and Mushroom Rice

Serves 4

1¼ cups easy-cook rice

2 tablespoons butter

4 skinless, boneless chicken breasts, each weighing about 5 oz, cut on the angle into 6 slices

1 teaspoon Dijon mustard

2 tablespoons tarragon wine vinegar or white wine vinegar

1¾ cups crème fraîche

4 tablespoons chopped tarragon

4 tablespoons olive oil

3¼ cups crimini mushrooms sliced

1 tablespoon wholegrain mustard

pepper

- Cook the rice in a large saucepan of lightly salted boiling water for 15 minutes, or until tender. Drain and set aside.

- Heat the butter in a large, heavy skillet over high heat. Add the chicken slices and cook for 10 minutes, or until golden. Stir in the Dijon mustard, then the wine vinegar, and cook for a few seconds until the vinegar burns off. Pour in the crème fraîche and chopped tarragon, reduce the heat, and stir well for 2 minutes until piping hot but not boiling. Season generously with pepper and set aside.

- Meanwhile, heat the oil in a large, heavy skillet over high heat and add the sliced mushrooms. Cook for 5 minutes, or until golden and cooked through. Add the drained rice and wholegrain mustard and stir-fry together for 2 minutes until piping hot. Divide the rice among 4 warmed serving plates, spoon the chicken on top, and serve.

Warm Chicken, Tarragon, and Mushroom Salad Place 2 tablespoons olive oil in a pan over high heat. Add 1 lb thinly sliced chicken tenders and 1½ cups quartered crimini mushrooms. Fry for 5 minutes, or until golden and cooked through, scattering with 2 tablespoons chopped tarragon for the final minute of cooking. Put 6 cups spinach and watercress in a large salad bowl, add the hot chicken and mushrooms, and toss together. Flavor a small quantity of mayonnaise with chopped tarragon and serve in a bowl on the side.

Baked Chicken Breasts with Tarragon Sauce Cut a slit in the side of 4 chicken breasts and insert a sprig of tarragon into each. Place in a roasting pan, season generously with salt and pepper, and put a walnut-sized lump of butter on top of each. Roast in a preheated oven at 400°F for 20–25 minutes, or until golden and cooked through. Meanwhile, make the sauce. Heat 2 tablespoons butter in a small saucepan, add 3 tablespoons all-purpose flour, and cook for a few seconds, stirring to blend. Remove the pan from the heat and add 2 tablespoons tarragon wine vinegar. Add 1¼ cups milk a little at a time. Return the pan to the heat and bring to a boil, stirring continually, until the sauce has boiled and thickened. Add ¼ cup chopped tarragon and ½ cup grated cheddar cheese. Stir well to melt the cheese and add ¼ cup plus 2 tablespoons heavy cream. Spoon the sauce over the chicken and serve with asparagus and new potatoes.

Quick Paella with Artichokes, Chorizo, and Green Beans

Serves 4

2 tablespoons olive oil
4 chicken drumsticks
3 oz chorizo, thinly sliced
1 small red onion, thinly sliced
1 cup paella rice
4 cups rich chicken stock
pinch of saffron threads
14 oz can artichoke hearts,
   drained and halved
3½ oz shelled jumbo shrimp
¼ lb green beans, trimmed

- Heat the oil in a large paella pan, wok, or skillet over high heat. Add the chicken drumsticks and cook, turning occasionally, for 5 minutes, or until golden. Add the chorizo and onion to the chicken and cook, stirring, for 2 minutes.

- Add the rice and toss to mix. Pour in all the stock and the saffron threads and bring to a boil. Reduce the heat, cover, and simmer, stirring occasionally, for 15 minutes.

- Add the artichokes, shrimp, and beans and stir well. Continue to cook, covered, for a further 5 minutes until all the ingredients are piping hot, cooked through, and tender.

1 Chicken, Artichoke, and Green Bean Bruschetta

Cut 4 thick slices on an angle from a ciabatta loaf and put them on the rack of a foil-lined broiler pan. Drizzle each with 1 tablespoon olive oil. Toast under a preheated hot broiler for 30 seconds on each side until golden and crisp. Keep warm. Place 1¼ cups passata in a small saucepan with a 14 oz can artichoke hearts, halved, a sliced cooked chicken breast, and ½ cup frozen green beans. Bring to a boil, reduce the heat, cover, and simmer for 3–4 minutes, or until piping hot. Stir through 3 tablespoons chopped parsley and serve on the ciabatta toast.

2 Chicken, Shrimp, and Chorizo Pilaf

Cook 1¼ cups quick-cooking white rice in a large saucepan of lightly salted boiling water for 12–15 minutes, or until tender, then drain. Meanwhile, heat 3 tablespoons olive oil in a large skillet over medium heat. Add 1 sliced red onion and ½ lb diced chicken meat with 3 oz sliced chorizo and cook for 8–10 minutes, or until golden. Add a 14 oz can artichokes, drained and halved, ¾ cup frozen peas, and ¾ cup chicken stock. Bring to a boil and cook for 2 minutes. Add the drained rice and toss together. Serve in warmed serving bowls with chopped parsley to garnish, if liked.

Chicken Breast with Blue Cheese and Mango Chutney

Serves 4

4 chicken breasts, each weighing about ¼ lb
1 tablespoon olive oil
4 oz Gorgonzola cheese, cut into 4 slices of the same size
4 generous tablespoons mango chutney
salt and pepper
salad, to serve

- Put the chicken breasts between 2 sheets of plastic wrap and beat them with a rolling pin until almost doubled in size and halved in thickness. Season with salt and pepper.

- Brush the chicken breasts with oil and cook, turning once, in a preheated ridged griddle pan for 7–8 minutes, or until golden and cooked through.

- Place on 4 warmed serving plates. Set a slice of Gorgonzola and 1 tablespoon of mango chutney on top of each portion. Serve with a simple salad.

Griddled Chicken Breasts with Blue Cheese Sauce Put 4 chicken breasts, each weighing about ¼ lb, between 2 sheets of plastic wrap and beat with a rolling pin until halved in thickness. Cook the chicken in a hot ridged griddle pan over a high heat, turning once, for 7–8 minutes, or until golden and cooked through. Meanwhile, melt 2 tablespoons butter in a saucepan, add 3 tablespoons flour, and cook for a few seconds. Remove from the heat and stir in 1¼ cups milk, a little at a time. Return to the heat and bring to a boil, stirring until thickened. Remove from the heat and add 4 oz crumbled Danish blue or Stilton cheese and stir until melted. Stir in 1 tablespoon thyme leaves. Spoon some sauce onto each chicken portion to serve.

Baked Chicken Breasts with Spicy Mangoes and Blue Cheese Use a sharp knife to slice 4 chicken breasts, each weighing about ¼ lb, almost in half along their length. Cut ¼ mango into thin slices and toss with 2 tablespoons mango chutney. Spoon the mixture into the 4 chicken breasts until they are completely full. Wrap each with 2 slices of prosciutto to hold it tightly together and keep the filling in place. Heat 1 tablespoon olive oil in a large, heavy skillet over high heat. Add the chicken and fry, turning once, for 5 minutes, or until pale golden on each side. Transfer to a roasting pan and bake in a preheated oven at 400°F for 20 minutes, or until golden and cooked through, placing a generous slice of Gorgonzola cheese on top of each chicken breast for the final 5 minutes of cooking. Serve with a simple salad, if liked.

Chicken, Apricot, and Almond Tagine

Serves 4

1 tablespoon olive oil
1 large onion, diced
8 boneless, skinless chicken
   thighs, cut into chunks
1 teaspoon ground cinnamon
1 cinnamon stick
1 teaspoon ground cumin
1 teaspoon ground coriander
½ teaspoon paprika
¾ cup dried apricots
¾ cup dried prunes
2½ cups chicken stock
1 teaspoon cornstarch
5 tablespoons chopped cilantro
scant ½ cup toasted blanched
   almonds
couscous, to serve (optional)

- Prepare the couscous, if using, by pouring boiling water over it according to the instructions on the package. Set aside.

- Meanwhile, prepare the tagine. Heat the oil in a large, heavy saucepan over high heat. Add the onion and chicken. Cook for 5 minutes, or until golden and beginning to soften. Add all the spices and cook, stirring, for 2 minutes.

- Add the dried fruit and stock. Bring to a boil then reduce the heat to a gentle simmer, and cook, uncovered, for a further 15 minutes, or until the chicken is tender and the dried fruit is soft yet still retaining its shape.

- Blend the cornstarch with 1 tablespoon of water and stir into the tagine to thicken. Add the chopped cilantro and almonds, stir, and heat for a further 1 minute before serving with couscous, if using.

---

1   Quick Couscous Salad with Moroccan

Flavors Prepare ½ cup lemon-and-cilantro-flavored couscous following the package instructions. Heat 1 tablespoon olive oil in a large skillet over high heat. Add 2 thinly sliced boneless, skinless chicken thighs, each weighing about 5 oz, and cook for 3–4 minutes. Add 1 bunch roughly diced scallions and cook for a further 4 minutes, or until the chicken is golden. Add to the couscous with 4 tablespoons chopped cilantro, ½ cup diced dried apricots, and a generous ½ cup toasted flaked almonds.

2   Moroccan-Style Chicken Soup

Put 1 tablespoon olive oil in a pan over high heat. Add 1 diced onion and 2 sliced boneless, skinless chicken thighs, each weighing about ¼ lb, for 5 minutes, or until golden. Add 1 teaspoon each ground cinnamon, ground cumin, ground coriander, and paprika and cook, stirring, for a further 1 minute. Add a 13½ oz can diced tomatoes and 2½ cups chicken stock and bring to a boil. Reduce the heat and simmer for 10 minutes before transferring to a food processor or blender. Blend, in batches if necessary,

until almost smooth. Return to the pan with a 15½ oz can rinsed and drained chickpeas and 3 tablespoons chopped fresh cilantro. Heat through for 2 minutes before ladling into warmed soup bowls and serving with crusty bread.

Roast Beet, Butternut Wedges, and Thyme Thighs

Serves 4

4 boneless chicken thighs
1¾ lb ready-prepared butternut squash wedges
10 oz raw beets (unpeeled), washed and cut into thin wedges
4 tablespoons olive oil
6 unpeeled garlic cloves
about 12 thyme sprigs
salt and pepper

- Open out each of the chicken thighs and season well with salt and pepper.

- Put the butternut squash and beet wedges into a large roasting pan and drizzle with the oil. Toss together with the garlic cloves and 8 of the thyme sprigs and season well. Put the remaining 4 thyme sprigs in the center of each of the boned chicken thighs, roll up, and secure with toothpicks.

- Roast in a preheated oven at 425°F for 20–25 minutes, or until the chicken is golden and cooked through and the vegetables are tender; the beets should still have a little bite. Serve hot with crusty buttered bread, if liked.

Chicken, Beet, and Cucumber Salad with Thyme Dressing

Cut 10 oz cooked beets into thin wedges, put them in a bowl with 3 cups watercress, and toss. Cut ½ cucumber in half, cut into chunks, and add to the salad with ½ lb flavored chicken slices (such as tikka). Drizzle with 5 tablespoons thyme-infused olive oil or 5 tablespoons olive oil mixed with 1 teaspoon dried thyme. Season with salt and pepper and serve.

Chicken, Sweet Potato, and Thyme Cannelloni

Heat 2 tablespoons olive oil in a large, heavy skillet over high heat. Add ¾ lb ground chicken and 1 small diced onion and cook for 5 minutes. Add 1 diced sweet potato and 2 tablespoons chopped rosemary leaves and cook for a further 5 minutes, or until the potato is beginning to soften. Spoon the mixture evenly onto 8 sheets of fresh lasagne, roll each one up, and place snugly in a shallow, ovenproof dish. Pour over 10 oz ready-made cheese sauce and scatter with ½ cup grated Parmesan cheese. Place under a preheated hot broiler and cook for 3–4 minutes, or until golden and bubbling.

Chicken Breasts with Crème Fraîche and Three-Mustard Sauce

Serves 4

4 chicken breasts, each weighing about 5 oz
1 tablespoon olive oil
1 tablespoon butter
1 scant cup crème fraîche
1 tablespoon wholegrain mustard
1 teaspoon English mustard
1 teaspoon Dijon mustard
3 tablespoons chopped parsley
pepper

To serve

green beans
new potatoes

- Heat the oil and butter in a large, heavy skillet over high heat. Add the chicken and cook, turning once, for 15 minutes or until golden and cooked through. Use a slotted turner to remove the chicken from the pan. Keep it warm.

- Add the crème fraîche to the pan with the mustards and stir for 2–3 minutes until warm but not boiled. Stir in the chopped parsley and season generously with pepper. Serve the chicken on warmed serving plates with the sauce spooned on top. Serve with green beans and buttered new potatoes, if liked.

Creamy Chicken Pan-Fry with Hot Mustard Sauce Place 2 tablespoons butter in a pan over high heat. Add ¾ lb diced chicken and cook for 7–8 minutes, or until golden. Add 1 tablespoon Dijon mustard, 2 teaspoons English mustard, and 1 teaspoon wholegrain mustard. Stir well, then add ¾ cup heavy cream. Stir and heat for 2 minutes until piping hot. Spoon the mixture onto warmed plates and garnish with parsley sprigs to serve.

Chicken and Mustard Lattice Pies Line a large cookie sheet with parchment paper. Unroll a 12 oz sheet of puff pastry. Cut the sheet in half lengthwise. (Keep the other half to use another time.) Cut half the pastry into 16 long strips, then cut each of these in half widthwise. Use each of the 8 strips to make 4 crisscross lattice patterns on the cookie sheet. Lightly brush with the beaten egg and bake in a preheated oven at 425°F for 15 minutes, or until golden and crisp. Meanwhile, heat 2 tablespoons butter in a large, heavy skillet over high heat. Add 1 lb diced chicken and cook for 15 minutes, or until golden and cooked through. Add 1 scant cup crème fraîche, 1 tablespoon wholegrain mustard, 1 teaspoon English, and 1 teaspoon Dijon mustard, and season generously with pepper. Heat through for 2–3 minutes until piping hot but not boiling. Add 3 tablespoons chopped parsley and stir through. Spoon the filling onto warmed serving plates. Place a lattice pastry on top of each portion to serve.

Asparagus and Pine Nut Filled Chicken with Mustard Sauce

Serves 4

4 chicken breasts, each weighing about ¼ lb

12 trimmed fine asparagus stems, halved lengthwise

2 tablespoons toasted pine nuts

2 tablespoons olive oil

1 tablespoon butter

1¾ cups crème fraîche

2 tablespoons Dijon mustard

salt and pepper

- Place the chicken breasts on a cutting board and slice them almost in half lengthwise. Lay 6 asparagus stems in each and scatter the pine nuts evenly among them. Season generously with salt and pepper, then close each breast and tie with kitchen string to hold in place.

- Heat the oil and butter in a large, heavy skillet over medium-high heat. Add the chicken and cook for 7–8 minutes on each side, or until golden and cooked through, covering the pan for the final 5 minutes of cooking.

- Meanwhile, mix together the crème fraîche and Dijon mustard and season well. Add the mixture to the pan with the chicken and gently heat, stirring, for 2 minutes or until hot. Serve the chicken with the mustard sauce on top, accompanied with cooked leeks and soybeans, if liked.

Broiled Chicken, Asparagus, and Pine Nuts on Spinach Salad Slice 2 chicken breasts and put in a bowl with 1 bunch of roughly chopped asparagus. Drizzle with 4 tablespoons olive oil and season with salt and pepper. Transfer to a large rack over a foil-lined broiler pan. Cook under a preheated hot broiler for 7–8 minutes, or until the chicken is cooked and the asparagus lightly charred and tender. Toss in a bowl with 7 oz fresh spinach and 4 tablespoons toasted pine nuts. Drizzle with balsamic vinegar to serve.

Creamy Chicken, Asparagus, and Pine Nut Tagliatelle Cook 8 oz dried tagliatelle in a large saucepan of lightly salted boiling water for 10 minutes, or until tender. Thinly slice 2 chicken breasts, each weighing about 5 oz. Heat 3 tablespoons olive oil in a large, heavy skillet over high heat. Add the chicken and cook for 5 minutes, or until beginning to brown. Add 1 roughly chopped bunch of asparagus and pan-fry for a further 5 minutes. Add 1¾ cups crème fraîche and 2 tablespoons Dijon mustard and heat, stirring, for 3–4 minutes.

Drain the pasta and toss into the pan with the chicken.

QuickCook
Healthy Feasts

Recipes listed by cooking time

Chicken Laksa with Noodles

Serves 4

1–2 tablespoons Thai red curry paste

4¼ cups hot chicken stock

10 oz cooked chicken, torn into strips

12 oz ready-cooked thin rice noodles

13½ fl oz can reduced-fat coconut milk

10 oz package prepared stir-fry vegetables

juice of 1 lime

small handful of fresh cilantro

salt and pepper

- Fry the curry paste in a large pan for 1 minute over medium heat. Add the hot stock, chicken, and noodles and simmer for 3 minutes.

- Add the coconut milk, bring back to a boil and stir in the prepared stir-fry vegetables. Simmer for 2 minutes, stir in the lime juice, and season with salt and pepper. Ladle into bowls and scatter with fresh cilantro to serve.

 Stir-Fried Chicken Noodles

Heat 1 tablespoon vegetable oil in a large skillet over high heat. Add 3 chicken breasts, each weighing 5 oz, cut into strips, 1 bunch of scallions cut into strips, 2 cups sugar snap peas, and 1 red pepper, cut into strips. Stir-fry for 6–7 minutes, then add 1–2 tablespoons Thai red curry paste and 2 × 5 oz packages of ready-cooked noodles. Heat through and scatter with chopped peanuts.

Thai Chicken Curry

Chop 3 skinless, boneless chicken breasts into pieces and stir-fry with 1–2 tablespoons Thai red curry paste and 1 tablespoon vegetable oil for 5 minutes. Add 2 cups chicken stock and simmer for 10 minutes before adding 13½ fl oz can coconut milk and 10 oz package prepared stir-fry vegetables. Garnish with fresh cilantro leaves and serve with jasmine rice.

Chicken Tacos

Serves 4

1 tablespoon vegetable oil
1 lb ground chicken
2 garlic cloves, crushed
2–3 tablespoons taco or fajita
   seasoning mix, to taste
juice of 1 lime
8 taco shells

To serve

tomato salsa
fat-free Greek-style yogurt
shredded crisp lettuce
grated low-fat cheddar cheese
lime wedges

- Heat the oil in a skillet over medium heat, add the ground chicken, and stir-fry, keeping the meat in clumps. Add the garlic and seasoning mix and continue cooking for 5 minutes, adding a little water if the mixture becomes too dry. Stir in the lime juice.

- Warm the taco shells according to the instructions on the package. Spoon in the ground chicken mixture and place some tomato salsa, yogurt, shredded lettuce, and grated cheese on top. Serve with lime wedges on the side.

Tex–Mex Chicken and Beans

Fry 1 lb ground chicken in 1 tablespoon sunflower oil over high heat with taco or fajita seasoning mix, to taste, for 5 minutes until clumpy and cooked. Add 8 fl oz passata and 7½ oz can kidney beans, rinsed and drained. Heat through and serve on thick slices of toast from a crusty loaf.

Mexican Chicken Burgers with Sweet Potato Wedges

Cut 2 sweet potatoes into thin wedges, toss in 1 tablespoon olive oil, season, and spread over a baking pan. Cook in a preheated oven at 425°F, turning occasionally, for 25 minutes or until tender. Meanwhile, mix 1 lb ground chicken with 1 crushed garlic clove and taco or fajita seasoning mix, to taste. Shape into 4 burgers and fry in 1 tablespoon oil for 8–10 minutes, turning once, or until browned and cooked through. Serve with tomato salsa, yogurt, crisp lettuce, and the sweet potato wedges.

Chicken Drumstick Jambalaya

Serves 4

1 tablespoon sunflower oil

8 chicken drumsticks, skinned

1 onion, diced

2 garlic cloves, crushed

2 celery sticks, sliced

1 red chile, seeded and diced

1 green pepper, cored, seeded, and diced

3 oz chorizo sausage, sliced

1¼ cups American long-grain rice

2 cups chicken stock

1 bay leaf

3 tomatoes, cut into wedges

dash of Tabasco sauce

salt and pepper

- Heat the oil in a large pan over high heat. Cut a few slashes across the thickest part of the drumsticks, add them to the skillet, and fry for 5 minutes, turning occasionally. Add the onion, garlic, celery, chile, and pepper and cook for a further 2–3 minutes, or until softened.

- Add the chorizo, fry briefly, then add the rice, stirring to coat the grains in the pan juices. Pour in the stock, add the bay leaf, and bring to a boil. Cover, reduce the heat, and simmer for 20 minutes, stirring occasionally, until the stock has been absorbed and the rice is tender.

- Stir in the tomatoes and Tabasco sauce and season to taste. Heat through for 3 minutes before serving.

---

1 Quick Chicken and Chorizo Stew

Pour a 10½ oz jar of ready-made tomato and roasted pepper pasta sauce into a saucepan. Add ½ lb chopped cooked chicken, 3 oz sliced chorizo, and a 15½ oz can of lima beans. Simmer for 5 minutes and serve with crusty bread.

2 Spanish Chicken with Spicy

Potatoes Cut 4 skinless, boneless chicken breasts into chunks and fry in 1 tablespoon olive oil with 1 sliced onion, 2 crushed garlic cloves, 2 sliced celery sticks, and 3 oz sliced chorizo sausages. Cook for 5 minutes, stirring. Add 1¼ cups canned diced tomatoes and a dash of Tabasco sauce and simmer for 10 minutes. Meanwhile, in a separate pan, fry a 14½ oz can of new potatoes, drained and halved, in1 tablespoon olive oil for 5 minutes, or until golden. Add ½ teaspoon smoked paprika and ¼ teaspoon cayenne pepper and cook for 2 minutes. Serve with the Spanish chicken.

Griddled Chicken with Cilantro Aïoli

Serves 4

2 teaspoons coarsely crushed
   black peppercorns
4 skinless, boneless chicken
   breasts, thinly sliced
1 tablespoon olive oil

For the cilantro aïoli

small bunch of cilantro, leaves
   only
1 garlic clove, peeled
2 teaspoons Dijon mustard
1 egg yolk
2 teaspoons white wine vinegar
¾ cup sunflower oil
salt and pepper

- Make the cilantro aioli. Reserve a few cilantro leaves for the garnish and place the rest in a small food processor or blender with the garlic, mustard, egg yolk, and vinegar. Blend until finely chopped. With the motor running, slowly drizzle in the oil until the mixture is smooth and thick. Season with salt and pepper.

- Scatter the crushed peppercorns over the chicken slices and drizzle with oil. Cook, in batches, on a preheated hot ridged griddle pan for 1–2 minutes on each side, or until cooked through and golden.

- Serve the warm chicken slices with mixed green salad leaves, grated beets, and the cilantro aïoli. Garnish with the reserved cilantro leaves.

Griddled Chicken and Tomato Sandwiches Thinly slice 3 skinless, boneless chicken breasts, season with salt and plenty of pepper, and drizzle with 1 tablespoon olive oil. Cut 4 tomatoes in half, season, and drizzle with a little oil. Cook the chicken and tomatoes, in batches, on a preheated hot ridged griddle for 1–2 minutes on each side, or until cooked and golden. Sandwich between slices of crusty whole-grain bread with arugula and ready-made roast garlic mayonnaise.

Griddled Chicken with Garlic Mayonnaise Thinly slice 4 skinless, boneless chicken breasts, season with 2 teaspoons coarsely crushed black peppercorns, and drizzle with 1 tablespoon olive oil. Cook, in batches, on a preheated hot ridged griddle pan for 1–2 minutes each side, or until cooked through and golden. Stir 1 crushed garlic clove into ¾ cup ready-made reduced-fat mayonnaise. Serve with mixed green salad leaves.

Chicken Minestrone

Serves 4

13½ oz can diced tomatoes
2½ cups chicken stock
¼ lb cooked chicken, chopped
1 zucchini, diced
1½ cups mixed frozen vegetables
3 oz mini pasta shapes
1 tablespoon ready-made pesto
salt and pepper

- Put the tomatoes, stock, chicken, zucchini, and frozen mixed vegetables in a saucepan. Bring to a boil, stirring, then add the pasta shapes and simmer for 5 minutes, or until the pasta is just al dente.

- Season with salt and pepper and stir in the pesto just before serving.

 Vegetable Chicken and Rice

Put a 13½ oz can diced tomatoes in a saucepan with 7 oz chopped cooked chicken, 1 diced zucchini, 1½ cups frozen mixed vegetables, and ½ cup chicken stock to heat through. Simmer for 5 minutes, add 1¼ cups long-grain rice, and simmer, stirring occasionally, for 10 minutes, or until the rice is cooked, adding a little boiling water if the mixture is too dry. Stir in 4 cups baby spinach until just wilted and serve.

Chicken and Vegetable

Casserole Cut 4 boneless, skinless chicken breasts in half lengthwise and fry in 1 tablespoon olive oil until browned on both sides. Add a 13½ oz can diced tomatoes, 1 diced zucchini, and 1 generous cup frozen mixed vegetables. Cover and simmer gently for 15 minutes, stir in 2 tablespoons ready-made pesto, and serve with cooked tagliatelle.

# Chicken and Eggplant Bake

Serves 4

1 eggplant, thinly sliced
olive oil cooking spray
6 skinless, boneless chicken
  thighs, chopped
10½ oz jar ready-made tomato
  and basil pasta sauce
5 oz mozzarella cheese, drained
  and diced
¾ cup fresh white bread crumbs
2 tablespoons freshly grated
  Parmesan cheese
salt and pepper

- Place the eggplant slices on a foil-lined broiler pan and lightly spray with olive oil cooking spray. Broil for about 5 minutes, turning once, or until tender.

- Meanwhile, lightly spray a nonstick skillet with oil and cook the chicken over high heat for 5 minutes, or until cooked through. Stir in the pasta sauce and bring to a boil.

- Place half the eggplant slices in the bottom of an ovenproof dish, pour the chicken and tomato mixture on top, and cover with the remaining eggplant. Mix together the mozzarella, bread crumbs, Parmesan, and seasoning and scatter evenly on the top. Bake in a preheated oven at 400°F for 15 minutes, or until the topping is golden and crisp.

Chicken, Eggplant, and Tomato Soup

Stir-fry 4 chopped skinless, boneless chicken thighs in 1 tablespoon olive oil with 1 diced eggplant for 5 minutes. Stir in 2½ cups ready-made tomato soup and heat through until hot. Serve with a swirl of low-fat yogurt.

Chicken and Eggplant Spaghetti

Fry 1 diced eggplant and 1 diced zucchini in 1 tablespoon sunflower oil with 4 chopped skinless, boneless chicken thighs for 5 minutes. Add a 10½ oz jar ready-made tomato and basil pasta sauce, bring to a boil, and simmer for 10 minutes.

Meanwhile, cook ½ lb spaghetti in lightly salted boiling water for 10 minutes, or until cooked. Drain, add to the tomato mixture with 2 tablespoons chopped parsley. Serve with freshly grated Parmesan cheese.

Chicken Pilau with Cauliflower, Spinach, and Green Beans

Serves 4

1 tablespoon sunflower oil
1 onion, diced
6 skinless, boneless chicken thighs, chopped
2 tablespoons korma curry paste
1½ cups basmati rice
4¼ cups chicken stock
1 small cauliflower, cut into florets
5 oz frozen spinach
1 generous cup green beans, trimmed and halved widthwise
2 carrots, coarsely grated
¼ cup flaked almonds, toasted
salt and pepper
low-fat natural yogurt, to serve

- Heat the oil in a large pan over medium heat. Add the onion and chicken and cook, stirring, for 5 minutes. Stir in the curry paste, rice, stock, cauliflower, and green beans. Bring to a boil, reduce the heat, cover, and simmer for 10 minutes, or until the stock has been absorbed and the rice and vegetables are tender.

- Stir in the grated carrots, heat through for 1 minute, and season with salt and pepper. Scatter with flaked almonds and serve with natural yogurt.

1 Curried Chicken and Rice

Heat 2 tablespoons korma paste in a pan, add 7 oz chopped cooked chicken, 1 generous cup frozen mixed vegetables, and about 4 tablespoons boiling water. Cover and cook for 5 minutes, stir in 1 lb ready-cooked pilau rice, and heat through for 3 minutes, stirring, until hot.

2 Creamy Chicken Curry with Cauliflower and Spinach

Fry 1 diced onion, 6 chopped skinless, boneless chicken thighs, and 1 small cauliflower, cut into florets, in 1 tablespoon sunflower oil for 5 minutes. Add 1½ cups sliced mushrooms, ¾ cup chicken stock, and 2 tablespoons mild curry paste. Simmer for 5 minutes, then stir in ½ generous cup low-fat Greek-style yogurt. Stir well, season with salt and pepper, and heat through. Add 3 cups baby spinach leaves and stir until wilted. Serve with rice or naan bread.

Lime and Sweet Chili Chicken with Mashed Sweet Potatoes

Serves 4

3 sweet potatoes, diced
1 tablespoon sweet chili sauce
1 tablespoon soy sauce
2 tablespoons lime juice
4 skinless, boneless chicken
    breasts, halved horizontally
2 teaspoons sesame oil
1 tablespoon sesame seeds
2 tablespoons reduced-fat spread
skim milk, to mix
salt and pepper
green beans, to serve

- Cook the sweet potatoes in a large saucepan of lightly salted boiling water for 15–20 minutes, or until tender.

- Meanwhile, in a large, shallow dish mix together the sweet chili sauce, soy sauce, and lime juice. Add the chicken breast halves and turn to coat in the mixture.

- Heat the sesame oil in a large, nonstick skillet, add the chicken, and fry for 5 minutes on each side, turning once, or until browned and cooked through. Add any remaining sauce mixture and scatter with the sesame seeds. Cook for a few more minutes.

- Drain the sweet potatoes and mash with the reduced-fat spread and a little milk until smooth. Season with salt and pepper. Serve with the sweet chili chicken and with green beans on the side.

Sticky Chili Chicken Lettuce Wraps

Toss ¾ lb chicken tenders in 2 tablespoons sweet chili sauce. Stir-fry in 2 teaspoons sesame oil for 5 minutes until cooked. Add a squeeze of lime juice and serve with crisp lettuce leaves to wrap the chicken. Serve with extra sweet chili sauce separately for dipping.

Lime and Sweet Chili Chicken Salad

Cut 4 skinless, boneless chicken breasts into strips and toss them in a mixture of 1 tablespoon sweet chili sauce, 1 tablespoon soy sauce, and 2 tablespoons lime juice. Stir-fry in 2 teaspoons sesame oil for 5 minutes. Serve on a bed on crisp shredded lettuce, thinly sliced cucumber, and a handful of roughly chopped fresh cilantro.

Chicken Couscous Salad

Serves 4

1½ cups couscous

1 cup hot chicken stock

15½ oz can chickpeas, drained

7 oz roasted peppers in oil from a jar, drained and diced (reserve 3 tablespoons of the oil)

½ cup cherry tomatoes, halved

4 tablespoons chopped mixed herbs, such as parsley, mint, and fresh cilantro

7 oz cooked barbecue-flavored chicken, chopped

1 tablespoon white wine vinegar

1 teaspoon Dijon mustard

salt and pepper

- Put the couscous in a heatproof bowl, pour over the hot stock, cover the bowl with a plate, and leave to stand for 5–8 minutes, or until the stock has been absorbed.

- Meanwhile, in a large bowl mix together the chickpeas, peppers, tomatoes, herbs, and chicken.

- In a small bowl mix together the oil from the peppers, the vinegar, and mustard. Season with salt and pepper. Uncover the couscous, fluff up with a fork, add the dressing and chicken mixture, and stir well to mix.

Pasta Salad
Cook 8 oz pasta shapes in lightly salted boiling water for 10 minutes or until just tender. Drain, rinse under cold water, and drain again. Add ½ cup halved cherry tomatoes, 3 tablespoons chopped mixed herbs, 4 oz roasted peppers from a jar, and 7 oz cooked chopped barbecue-flavored chicken. Mix together with 4 tablespoons ready-made French dressing, ½ cup black olives, and a handful of arugula.

Stuffed Peppers
Halve and seed 4 red peppers and roast in a preheated oven at 425°F for 20 minutes until softened and lightly charred. Meanwhile, soak 1 cup couscous in ¾ cup hot chicken stock for 10 minutes, or until the stock has been absorbed. Fluff up with a fork and stir in ½ cup halved cherry tomatoes, 3 tablespoons chopped mixed parsley, mint, and cilantro, 6 oz chopped cooked barbecue-flavored chicken and 3 oz diced haloumi cheese. Divide the mixture among the pepper halves, drizzle with a little olive oil, and finish under the grill for 5 minutes to brown.

Saucy Lemon Chicken with Greens

Serves 4

2 teaspoons sesame oil

4 skinless, boneless chicken
   breasts

1 red chile, seeded and diced

finely grated zest of 1 lemon

8 tablespoons lemon juice

2 heads of bok choy, halved

1 tablespoon cornstarch, mixed to
   a paste with 2 tablespoons
   water

- Heat the sesame oil in a large, heavy skillet over medium heat. Add the chicken breasts and fry them, turning once, for 5 minutes, or until browned. Add the chile to the pan with the lemon zest and juice. Cover and simmer for 15 minutes or until the chicken is cooked.

- Meanwhile, steam or lightly cook the bok choy in a little lightly salted boiling water until just tender.

- Remove the chicken from the pan and keep warm. Stir the cornstarch paste into the pan juices and bring to a boil, stirring until thickened and adding a little water if the sauce is too thick. Serve the chicken with the bok choy and the lemon sauce poured on the top.

Lemon Noodle Chicken

Stir-fry 7 oz chicken tenders in 2 teaspoons sesame oil for 5 minutes or until browned and cooked. Add 1 scant cup lemon stir-fry sauce, 10 oz prepared mixed stir-fry vegetables, and 5 oz ready-cooked noodles. Cook, stirring continuously, for 5 minutes and serve.

Pineapple Chicken

Stir-fry 4 skinless, boneless chicken breasts cut into strips in 1 teaspoon sesame oil for 5 minutes, or until golden and cooked. Drain an 8½ oz can pineapple chunks in juice, reserving the juice. Add the pineapple, 1 seeded and diced red chile, and 2 heads of bok choy, leaves separated, to the pan. Cook for 3 minutes until hot. Mix a little of the reserved pineapple juice with 1 tablespoon cornstarch to make a smooth paste, then stir in the remaining juice. Pour into the pan and cook, stirring, until thickened. Serve with noodles.

Spanish Chicken and Potato Stew

Serves 4

2 tablespoon olive oil
4 boneless, skinless chicken
   thighs, thinly sliced
1 lb potatoes, diced
1 red onion, sliced
1 green pepper, cored, seeded,
   and thinly sliced
1 small red chile, minced
1 garlic clove, crushed
1 tablespoon smoked paprika
13½ oz can diced tomatoes
3 large tomatoes, roughly diced
1¼ cups chicken stock
salt and pepper
crusty bread, to serve

- Heat the oil in a pan over high heat. Add the chicken, potatoes, onion, green pepper, chile, garlic, and paprika. Cook, stirring, for 10 minutes.

- Add the canned tomatoes, fresh tomatoes, and stock and bring to a boil, then reduce the heat and simmer, uncovered, for 6–7 minutes, or until the chicken and potatoes are cooked through and the tomatoes have softened. Season with salt and pepper and serve with crusty bread to mop up the juices.

Chicken and Chorizo Pasta

Fry 6 chopped skinless, boneless chicken thighs with 4 oz sliced chorizo for 3 minutes over high heat. Stir in a 10½ oz jar ready-made tomato and chili pasta sauce and simmer for 5 minutes. Meanwhile, cook 12 oz tagliatelle in a large saucepan of lightly salted boiling water. Drain the tagliatelle, add the sauce, stir well, and serve.

Chili Chicken

Chop 8 skinless, boneless chicken thighs and fry over medium heat in 1 tablespoon olive oil with 1 diced onion, 1 diced green pepper, and 2 teaspoons chili powder for 5 minutes. Add 1 tablespoon tomato paste with a 15 oz can cannellini beans, rinsed and drained, and a 13½ oz can diced tomatoes. Make a tomato salsa by mixing 2 diced tomatoes, 1 small diced red onion, and 1 tablespoon chopped parsley. Serve the chicken with the salsa, rice, and fat-free Greek yogurt.

Mixed Mushroom, Herb, and Chicken Frittata

Serves 4

1 tablespoon olive oil

1 skinless, boneless chicken breast, sliced

2¼ cups mixed mushrooms, such as chestnut, oyster, and shiitake, sliced

1 red pepper, cored, seeded, and diced

4 scallions, thinly sliced

8 eggs

3 tablespoons chopped herbs, such as parsley, chives, and thyme

½ cup low-fat soft cheese with chives

salt and pepper

- Heat the oil in a large, nonstick skillet over high heat. Add the chicken, mushrooms, red pepper, and scallions and cook for 5 minutes, or until the chicken is cooked and the vegetables are tender.

- Beat the eggs with the herbs and season with salt and pepper. Pour into the pan over the chicken and vegetables and cook gently for about 5 minutes, or until set around the edges.

- Scatter spoonfuls of the soft cheese over the top of the frittata and place the pan under a broiler preheated to medium. Cook until the frittata is just set and the top is golden. Serve warm or cold.

Garlic Mushroom and Chicken Pizza

Fry 2¼ cups sliced mixed mushrooms in 1 tablespoon sunflower oil for 3 minutes. Stir in 1 chopped cooked chicken breast. Spread pizza sauce onto a ready-made pizza crust, spoon the mushrooms evenly on top, and scatter with spoonfuls of low-fat garlic and herb soft cheese. Broil until melted and golden.

Pasta Bake

In a large skillet, fry 2 sliced skinless, boneless chicken breasts in 1 tablespoon sunflower oil with 2¼ cups mixed sliced mushrooms, 1 diced red pepper, and 4 diced scallions. Stir in ½ cup low-fat soft cheese with chives and 1 scant cup reduced-fat crème fraîche. Heat to make a sauce, adding a little hot water if too thick. Season with salt and pepper, add 3 tablespoons chopped mixed herbs, and stir in 8 oz cooked pasta shapes. Pour into a heatproof dish, scatter with a little freshly grated Parmesan cheese, and broil for 5 minutes until golden.

Baked Chicken and Shrimp Egg Rolls

Serves 4

7 oz prepared mixed stir-fry vegetables

1 tablespoon sesame oil

1 red chile, seeded and diced

½ inch piece fresh ginger root, peeled and grated

7 oz cooked chicken, chopped

4 oz small shelled shrimp, thawed if frozen, diced

2 tablespoons Chinese stir-fry sauce, any flavor

6 sheets filo pastry

2 tablespoons sunflower oil

salt and pepper

teriyaki sauce, for dipping

- Roughly chop the stir-fry vegetables to make the pieces slightly smaller, then place in a bowl. Add the sesame oil, chile, ginger root, chicken, shrimp, and sauce. Season with salt and pepper and mix well.

- Work with 1 sheet of filo pastry at a time and keep the rest of the sheets covered with plastic wrap to stop them from drying out. Cut each sheet in half widthwise and put one-twelfth of the chicken mixture at one end of each strip. Roll it up, tucking in the ends as you roll. Place on a cookie sheet and brush with a little sunflower oil. Repeat with remaining pastry and filling to make 12 rolls.

- Bake in a preheated oven at 400°F for 15 minutes, or until golden and crisp. Serve warm with teriyaki sauce for dipping.

Teriyaki Chicken Rolls

Warm 12 pancakes (the type used for crispy duck) in the microwave according to the instructions on the package. Fill with ½ lb cooked chicken cut into strips, 6 scallions, cut into fine strips, and ¼ cucumber, cut into sticks. Pour in a little teriyaki sauce, roll up, and serve.

Chicken and Shrimp Filo Tarts

Brush 4 sheets of filo pastry with a little sunflower oil, fold each sheet in half widthwise, and scrunch the edges roughly to make a circle with a ruffled edge. Place on two cookie sheets, brush with a little more oil, and bake in a preheated oven at 400°F for 10 minutes, or until golden and crisp. Meanwhile, stir-fry, 1 diced red chile, ½ inch piece peeled ginger root, grated, 7 oz diced cooked chicken, 4 oz shelled shrimp, and 7 oz prepared mixed stir-fry vegetables in 1 tablespoon vegetable oil. Add 2–3 tablespoons teriyaki sauce and heat through. Spoon into the filo tart cases and drizzle with a little extra teriyaki sauce to serve.

Chicken Ratatouille

Serves 4

8 small, skinless chicken thighs
1 tablespoon olive oil
1 onion, diced
1 eggplant, cut into bite-size
   chunks
1 green pepper, cored, seeded,
   and cut into bite-size chunks
1 red pepper, cored, seeded, and
   cut into bite-size chunks
2 zucchini, diced
1 garlic clove, crushed
13½ oz can diced tomatoes
pinch of superfine sugar
handful of basil leaves, roughly
   torn
salt and pepper

- Cut a couple of slashes across each chicken thigh and season with salt and pepper. Heat the oil in a large deep skillet, add the chicken, and cook over high heat for 5 minutes, turning occasionally.

- Add the onion, eggplant, peppers, zucchini, and garlic and cook for 10 minutes, or until softened, adding a little water if the mixture becomes too dry.

- Add the tomatoes and sugar, season with salt and pepper, and bring to a boil, stirring. Reduce the heat, cover, and simmer for 15 minutes, stirring occasionally. Stir in the basil and serve.

1 Chicken Ratatouille Pie

Heat 2 x 14 oz cans or jars of ratatouille in a saucepan. Add ½ lb chopped cooked chicken, heat through, and tip into a heatproof dish. Scatter with ½ ciabatta loaf torn into pieces and cover evenly with 2 tablespoons freshly grated Parmesan cheese. Broil for a few minutes to toast the bread.

2 Chicken Ratatouille

with Lentils Chop 4 skinless, boneless chicken breasts and fry in 1 tablespoon olive oil for 5 minutes. Add 1 diced eggplant, 2 diced zucchini, 2 diced roasted red peppers from a can or jar, a 13½ oz can diced tomatoes with garlic and herbs, and a 13 oz can green lentils, rinsed and drained. Bring to a boil, reduce the heat, cover, and simmer for 10 minutes. Scatter with chopped basil to serve.

Chicken Tikka Kebabs with Red Onion Relish

Serves 4

¾ cup low-fat plain yogurt

2 tablespoons tandoori or tikka paste

4 tablespoons lemon juice

4 skinless, boneless chicken breasts, cut into bite-size pieces

1 red onion, finely sliced

2 tablespoons chopped fresh cilantro

1 tablespoon olive oil

basmati rice, to serve

- Mix together the yogurt, tandoori or tikka paste, and half the lemon juice. Add the chicken and stir well. Thread onto skewers and place on a foil-lined broiler pan.

- Cook under a preheated hot broiler, turning occasionally, for 8–10 minutes, or until the chicken is cooked and lightly charred at the edges.

- Meanwhile, make the relish by mixing together the red onion, fresh cilantro, olive oil, and remaining lemon juice. Serve with the chicken tikka and rice.

Chicken Tikka Wraps

Put pieces of cooked chicken tikka on a soft flour tortilla, add shredded scallions, crisp lettuce, and cucumber sticks. Spoon on some ready-made tzatziki and roll up to serve.

Chicken Tikka Masala

Prepare the chicken as above. While it is cooking make the masala sauce. Fry 1 diced onion in 1 tablespoon vegetable oil, add 1 crushed garlic clove, 1 teaspoon ground cumin, 1 teaspoon ground coriander, and 1½ teaspoons garam masala.

Stir in a 13½ oz can diced tomatoes and simmer for 10 minutes. Remove from the heat and stir in ¾ cup fat-free Greek-style yogurt. Reheat gently but do not let the mixture boil. Take the cooked chicken tikka off the skewers and stir into the sauce. Serve with red onion relish and rice.

Spiced Roast Chicken with Lime

Serves 4

8 small chicken thighs, skinned
1 tablespoon harissa
4 tablespoons clear honey
2 limes, cut into wedges
1 red pepper, cored seeded,
    and cut large chunks
2 zucchini, cut into chunks
1 onion, cut into wedges
10 oz new potatoes, halved if
    large
1 tablespoon olive oil
salt and pepper

- Cut a few slashes across each chicken thigh. Mix together the harissa and honey and rub all over the chicken thighs. Place in a roasting pan large enough to spread everything out in a single layer, with the lime wedges, red pepper, zucchini, onion, and potatoes.

- Drizzle over the oil, season with salt and pepper, and roast in a preheated oven at 425°F for 25 minutes, turning occasionally, or until the chicken is cooked and the vegetables are tender. Serve with the juice of the lime wedges squeezed over the chicken.

---

1 **Harissa Chicken Pitas**

Coat ¾ lb chicken tenders in 1 tablespoon harissa and 1 tablespoon clear honey. Stir-fry in 1 tablespoon sunflower oil for 5 minutes, or until cooked through. Pile into warmed pita bread with some shredded crisp lettuce, grated carrots, and spoonfuls of ready-made reduced-fat hummus.

2 **Pan-Fried Spicy Chicken**

Cut 8 small skinless, boneless chicken thighs into strips and coat in a mixture of 1 tablespoon harissa and 1 tablespoon clear honey. Heat 1 tablespoon sunflower oil in a large skillet, add the chicken, and fry over medium heat for 5 minutes. Add 1 seeded and diced pepper, 2 diced zucchini, 1 onion, cut into

 thin wedges, and 2 limes, cut into wedges. Cook for 10 minutes, stirring occasionally, or until the chicken is cooked and the vegetables are tender. Serve with new potatoes.

Coconut and Cilantro Chicken

Serves 4

1 tablespoon sunflower oil

4 skinless, boneless chicken breasts

1 bunch of scallions, trimmed and diced

¾ cup reduced-fat coconut milk

1 tablespoon nam pla (Thai fish sauce)

juice of 1 lime

1 teaspoon cornstarch

small handful of fresh cilantro leaves, roughly chopped

handful of coconut shavings

salt and pepper

To serve

Thai sticky rice

snow peas

- Heat the oil in a large skillet, add the chicken breasts, and cook, turning once, for 5 minutes, or until browned. Remove the chicken from the pan and slice, then return to the pan. Add the scallions, coconut milk, fish sauce, and lime juice. Season with salt and pepper, cover the pan, and simmer gently for 20 minutes or until the chicken is cooked.

- Mix the cornstarch with 1 tablespoon water and add to the sauce to thicken if necessary. Stir in half the cilantro leaves and scatter the rest over the top along with the coconut shavings. Serve with Thai sticky rice and snow peas.

Coconut, Cilantro, and Chicken Salad
Mix 10 oz sliced cooked chicken with 2 handfuls of fresh cilantro leaves, 1¼ cups bean sprouts, 2 cups snow peas, a handful of coconut shavings, and ¼ diced cucumber. Drizzle with 4 tablespoons reduced-fat ready-made Thai-style salad dressing before serving.

Coconut and Cilantro Chicken Soup Heat a 13½ fl oz can reduced-fat coconut milk with 2 cups chicken stock. Add 3 chopped skinless, boneless chicken breasts, 2 tablespoons Thai fish sauce, 1 bunch of diced scallions, and a handful of roughly chopped fresh cilantro leaves. Simmer for 15 minutes.

Add the juice of 1 lime and season with salt and pepper. Scatter with coconut shavings and some extra cilantro leaves to serve.

Warm Chicken, Pine Nut, and Raisin Salad

Serves 4

2 tablespoons pine nuts

4 skinless, boneless chicken breasts, halved horizontally

2–3 teaspoons paprika

1 tablespoon olive oil

handful of radicchio leaves

3½ oz mixed salad leaves

1 red onion, thinly sliced

4 tablespoons sherry vinegar

2 teaspoons Dijon mustard

2 tablespoons clear honey

½ cup raisins

salt and pepper

- Heat a nonstick skillet until hot. Add the pine nuts and dry-fry, stirring continuously, until golden, being careful not to let them burn. Tip them out of the pan onto a plate.

- Lightly dust the chicken breast halves with paprika and season with salt and pepper. Place the oil in the pan over medium heat. Add the chicken breasts and fry, turning occasionally, for about 10 minutes, or until cooked through.

- Meanwhile, mix together the radicchio, salad leaves, and red onion and place on serving plates. Remove the chicken from the pan and stir the vinegar, mustard, and honey into the pan juices. Heat though and add the raisins and pine nuts. Pour the warm dressing onto the salad and arrange the chicken on top to serve.

Paprika Chicken Wraps

Dust ¾ lb chicken tenders with 1 teaspoon smoked paprika. Fry in a little olive oil over high heat for 3 minutes until cooked. Stir in 1 tablespoon sherry vinegar and 1 teaspoon Dijon mustard, season with salt and pepper, and pile onto soft tortilla wraps with mixed salad leaves, including peppery arugula or watercress, and thinly sliced red onion. Roll up and serve warm.

Chicken, Raisin and Pine Nut Pilau

Cook 1¼ cups basmati rice in lightly salted boiling water for 10 minutes, or according to the instructions on the package. Cut 4 skinless, boneless chicken breasts into bite-size pieces and fry in 1 tablespoon olive oil with 1 teaspoon smoked paprika and 1 thinly sliced red onion for 5 minutes. Add the drained rice with 4 cups baby spinach, 2 tablespoons raisins, and 2 tablespoons pine nuts. Season and stir well to mix.

CHI-HEAL-ZYM

Herby Quinoa with Lemon and Chicken

Serves 4

1¼ cups quinoa
1 tablespoon olive oil
1 onion, diced
1 garlic clove, crushed
4 skinless, boneless chicken
   breasts, sliced
1 teaspoon ground coriander
½ teaspoon ground cumin
½ cup dried cranberries
¾ cup no-need-to-soak dried
   apricots, diced
4 tablespoons chopped parsley
4 tablespoons chopped mint
finely grated zest of 1 lemon
salt and pepper

- Cook the quinoa in a pan of lightly salted boiling water for 15 minutes until tender, then drain.

- Meanwhile, heat the oil in a large skillet over medium heat, add the onion and cook, stirring, for 5 minutes to soften. Add the garlic, chicken, coriander, and cumin and cook for a further 8–10 minutes, or until the chicken is cooked.

- Season the quinoa with salt and pepper. Add the chicken mixture, cranberries, apricots, herbs, and lemon zest. Stir well and serve warm or cold.

Chicken and Apricot Moroccan Couscous Put a generous ½ cup Moroccan-flavored couscous in a large bowl, cover with boiling water, cover the bowl with a plate, and leave to stand for 8 minutes. When all the water has been absorbed, stir in ½ lb chopped cooked chicken, 1 cup no-need-to-soak apricots, and a generous ¾ cup canned chickpeas, rinsed and drained.

Cilantro Couscous with Lemon and Chicken Put 1 generous cup couscous in a bowl, just cover with boiling water, cover the bowl with a plate, and leave to stand for 10 minutes. Meanwhile, fry 1 diced onion, 1 crushed garlic clove, and 4 chopped skinless, boneless chicken breasts in 1 tablespoon olive oil for 10 minutes or until the chicken is cooked. When the couscous has absorbed all the water, fluff it up with a fork, season, and stir in the chicken mixture with 4 tablespoons chopped fresh cilantro, the grated zest of 1 lemon, and 3 tablespoons raisins.

Chicken Koftas

Serves 4

1 lb ground chicken
2 garlic cloves, crushed
1 teaspoon ground cumin
2 teaspoons ground coriander
2 teaspoons fresh cilantro
1 scant cup fat-free
   Greek-style yogurt
1 tablespoon mint sauce
¼ cucumber, coarsely grated
   and squeezed to remove
   excess liquid
salt and pepper

- Put the ground chicken, garlic, cumin, ground coriander, and fresh cilantro in a bowl. Season with salt and pepper and mix well to combine.

- Using wet hands, make 12 evenly sized sausage shapes from the mixture and thread onto skewers, pressing firmly. Broil for 10 minutes, turning occasionally, until cooked through and browned.

- Meanwhile, mix together the yogurt, mint sauce, and cucumber. Take the koftas off the skewers and stuff into warmed pita breads along with some salad leaves and the yogurt dressing to serve.

Spiced Ground Chicken with Pita

Bread Fry 1 lb ground chicken in 1 tablespoon sunflower oil over high heat with 1 teaspoon garlic paste, 1 teaspoon ground cumin, 2 teaspoons ground coriander, and 1 teaspoon dried oregano. Add a little water to keep the mixture moist. Then add ¾ cup frozen peas. Cook for 8 minutes and serve with warmed pita bread and ready-made raita or tzatziki.

Quick Moussaka

Fry 1 lb ground chicken in 1 tablespoon sunflower oil in a skillet over medium until browned. Add 1 crushed garlic clove, 1 teaspoon ground cumin, 2 teaspoons ground coriander and a 13½ oz can diced tomatoes. Simmer for 10 minutes. Meanwhile, thinly slice 1 eggplant, brush with a little oil, and cook in a hot skillet for 2 minutes each side. Add the mixture to a baking dish and arrange the eggplant slices on top. Cover with a generous ¾ cup fat-free Greek-style yogurt whisked with 1 egg. Put the dish under a medium broiler and cook until golden and bubbling on top. Serve with a green salad.

Stir-Fried Chicken with Basil

Serves 2

1 tablespoon vegetable oil

2 shallots, sliced

1 red chile, seeded and sliced

1 garlic clove, sliced

¾ lb chicken tenders

1 tablespoon nam pla
  (Thai fish sauce)

1 teaspoon soy sauce

small handful of basil leaves

toasted coconut flakes, to garnish
  (optional)

- Heat the oil in a wok or large skillet over medium heat. Add the shallots, chile, and garlic and cook for 1 minute. Remove with a slotted spoon and keep warm.

- Add the chicken to the pan, stir-fry for 5 minutes, or until cooked and beginning to brown. Return the shallot mixture to the pan, then add the fish sauce, soy sauce, and basil and cook for 1 minute, or until the basil starts to wilt. Scatter with toasted coconut flakes, if using, and serve.

Chicken and Basil Soup Place 2 diced shallots, 1 diced red chile, 1 crushed garlic clove, and ½ lb chicken tenders in 2 cups hot chicken stock. Simmer for 10 minutes, then add 5 oz ready-cooked noodles, 1 tablespoon Thai fish sauce, 1 teaspoon soy sauce, and a small handful of basil leaves. Simmer for 5 minutes. Scatter with toasted flaked coconut and serve.

Egg Rolls Brush 4 sheets of filo pastry with a little oil. Prepare the stir-fried chicken as above and spoon one-quarter of the mixture onto each sheet and roll up to make 4 parcels, tucking the ends in as you go. Brush with a little oil, scatter with sesame seeds, and bake in a preheated oven at 425°F for 10 minutes, or until crisp and golden. Serve with sweet chili sauce separately for dipping.

Chicken Roasted with Lemon, Olives, and Saffron

Serves 4

pinch of saffron threads
4 chicken drumsticks and
4 small chicken thighs, skinned
1 lemon, halved
2 tablespoon clear honey
¾ cup dry white wine
¾ cup green olives
salt and pepper
2 tablespoons roughly chopped
   flat-leaf parsley, to garnish

- Soak the saffron in 1 tablespoon boiling water. Cut a couple of slashes across the top of each piece of chicken and season with salt and pepper. Spread out the chicken in a large roasting pan or ovenproof dish and squeeze the juice from the lemon halves over the chicken.

- Drizzle with the honey, pour in the saffron threads and soaking water, and add the white wine. Roast in a preheated oven at 425°F for 20 minutes, basting with the juices occasionally. Add the olives and roast for a further 5 minutes, or until the chicken is cooked.

- Scatter with parsley and serve with new potatoes and green beans.

1 Lemon Chicken Stir-Fry

Heat 1 tablespoon sunflower oil in a wok or large skillet, add ¾ lb chicken tenders, and stir-fry over high heat for 5 minutes. Add 1 tablespoon clear honey, 4 tablespoons lemon juice, 4 tablespoons dry white wine, and ¾ cup green olives. Heat through for 2 minutes, season, and serve with ready-made couscous and a salad.

2 Roasted Chicken Breasts with Olives and Couscous

Soak a pinch of saffron threads in 1 tablespoon boiling water. Cut 4 skinless, boneless chicken breasts into 3 pieces each and place them in a roasting pan with 2 halved lemons. Drizzle with 1 tablespoon clear honey, the saffron and soaking water, and ¾ cup dry white wine. Season with salt and pepper and roast in a preheated oven at 425°F for 15 minutes, or until the chicken is cooked. Stir in ¾ cup green olives, scatter with 2 tablespoons chopped parsley and serve with couscous.

 # Yogurt Chicken with Greek Salad

Serves 4

¾ cup fat-free Greek yogurt
1 garlic clove, crushed
2 tablespoons olive oil
finely grated zest and juice of
  1 lemon
1 teaspoon ground cumin
4 skinless, boneless chicken
  breasts, cut into bite-size
  chunks
½ cucumber, diced
1 red onion, sliced
4 tomatoes, cut into slim wedges
16 black olives
1¼ cups feta cheese, crumbled
1 small romaine lettuce, torn

For the dressing

1 tablespoon lemon juice
2 tablespoons olive oil
1 tablespoon chopped fresh
  oregano or ½ teaspoon dried
  oregano

- Soak 8 small wooden skewers in water and preheat the broiler to high. In a bowl, mix together the yogurt, garlic, olive oil, lemon zest and juice, and cumin. Add the chicken, stir well, and thread onto 8 skewers. Place on a foil-lined broiler pan.

- Place under a preheated hot broiler and cook for 10 minutes, turning occasionally, or until the chicken is cooked and beginning to char in places.

- Meanwhile, in a salad bowl mix together the cucumber, onion, tomatoes, olives, feta, and lettuce.

- Make the dressing by whisking together the lemon juice, oil, and fresh or dried oregano. Pour the dressing onto the salad, toss to coat, and serve alongside the chicken skewers.

---

1   **Broiled Yogurt Chicken and Spinach Ciabatta** Prepare the chicken skewers as above. Split a ciabatta loaf lengthwise and spread with mayonnaise. Place a handful of baby spinach leaves on top, a few teaspoons of tomato chili jam, and then the hot chicken skewers, and serve.

 3   **Yogurt Chicken and Bulghur Wheat Salad** Prepare the chicken skewers as above. While they are cooking put ½ cup bulghur wheat in a pan with 1¾ cups boiling water. Cover and simmer for 15 minutes until the liquid has been absorbed. Cool slightly before mixing together with ½ diced cucumber, 1 sliced red onion, 4 diced tomatoes, 16 black olives, 1¼ cups crumbled feta cheese, and 2 tablespoons each of chopped parsley and chopped mint.

Chicken with Cashews and Oyster Sauce

Serves 2

generous ¼ cup unsalted cashews

1 teaspoon sesame oil

2 skinless, boneless chicken breasts, cut into strips

1 garlic clove, crushed

½ inch piece fresh ginger root, peeled and grated

1½ cups oyster mushrooms, sliced

4 scallions, thickly sliced diagonally

2 cups frozen soybeans

6 tablespoons oyster sauce

- Heat a wok or large skillet until hot and add the cashews. Cook, stirring, for 1 minute, or until golden, being careful not to let them burn. Transfer to a plate and set aside.

- Put the oil in the pan, add the chicken strips, and stir-fry for 3 minutes, or until browned and cooked through.

- Add the garlic, ginger root, mushrooms, and scallions. Cook for 2 minutes, or until the mushrooms and onions are just tender. Add the soybeans and oyster sauce, bring to a boil, and simmer for 2 minutes. Add a little water if the mixture is too dry. Scatter with the toasted cashews and serve.

Ginger Chicken and Rice Stir-Fry

Cook 2 chopped skinless, boneless chicken breasts in a large skillet with 1 teaspoon sunflower oil, 1 teaspoon garlic paste, 1 teaspoon ginger paste, 4 sliced scallions, and 2 cups frozen soybeans. Add 8 oz ready-cooked egg-fried rice and a dash each of sweet chili sauce and soy sauce. Stir-fry until hot.

Lemon Chicken with Cashews

Toast a generous ¼ cup unsalted cashews in a dry skillet or wok until golden. Remove from the pan, then heat 1 teaspoon sunflower oil and stir-fry 2 skinless, boneless chicken breasts, cut into strips, for 3 minutes. Add 1 crushed garlic clove, ½ inch piece fresh ginger root, peeled and grated, 1 diced red chile, 4 scallions, sliced on the angle, and 2 cups frozen soybeans. Stir-fry for 5 minutes then add 4 tablespoons chicken stock, 4 tablespoons lemon juice, 1 teaspoon soy sauce, and 1 teaspoon cornstarch mixed to a paste with a little water. Stir until thickened, scatter with the cashews, and serve.

Index

Page references in *italics* indicate photographs

Acknowledgments

Recipes by Emma Jane Frost
Executive Editor Eleanor Maxfield
Senior Editor Sybella Stephens
Copy Editor Lydia Darbyshire
Art Direction Tracy Killick for Tracy Killick Art Direction and Design
Original design concept www.gradedesign.com
Designer Sally Bond for Tracy Killick Art Direction and Design
Photographer Lis Parsons
Home Economist Emma Jane Frost
Prop Stylist Liz Hippisley
Production Caroline Alberti